# Tom Dodge Talks About Texas

## Radio Vignettes and Other Observations 1989-1999

# Tom Dodge

D1413089

REPUBLIC OF TEXAS PRESS

*Dallas • Lanham • Boulder • New York • Toronto • Plymouth, UK*

Published by Republic of Texas Press
An imprint of The Rowman & Littlefield Publishing Group, Inc.
4501 Forbes Boulevard, Suite 200
Lanham, MD 20706
http://www.rlpgtrade.com

10 Thornbury Road
Plymouth PL6 7PP
United Kingdom

Distributed by NATIONAL BOOK NETWORK

**Library of Congress Cataloging-in-Publication Data available**

ISBN 13: 978-1-55622-779-0 (pbk: alk. paper)

<sub></sub> The paper used in this publication meets the minimum requirements of American
National Standard for Information Sciences—Permanence of Paper for Printed Library
Materials, ANSI/NISO Z39.48-1992.

Manufactured in the United States of America.

# Dedication

To Brenda, with love,

and to the memory of Jack Mann and
Helen Mann Hollingsworth.

*Tom Dodge consistently demonstrates there are still decent people who genuinely care about what happens to other people. When he was teaching English at Mountain View College, Tom encouraged his students to trust their own ability to figure things out. His regular radio essays continue this theme and are demonstrations of Tom's "common sense in uncommon abundance" (wisdom).*

Bob Martin—former student

*We live in a time when it seems the only Texana we have is disappearing with the Marlborough Man. Tom Dodge rises as a true Texas hero and preserves our Southern heritage. Our God given right to "Think diffr'nt from other folks, hell, to think at all." I for one am thankful for his insights into the Real Texas way of thinking.*

*He is the only Greek scholar I know personally...and I miss the ol' goat.*

Judith Prueitt—former student

# Contents

Contents

# Contents

# Preface

*Tom Dodge Talks About Texas* is a presumptuous title, I know. When Ginnie Bivona, my editor, came up with it, of course I blustered. "Texas is a big place. It's over nine hundred miles across, has mountains, forests, deserts, more shoreline than many countries—more of everything than many countries. It has nearly twenty million people. I doubt that I know a hundred of them very well. I am not a student of Texas history. I have lived in Texas all my life, but in only four small towns—each with a population of less than fifteen thousand. My only association with cattle is that I've eaten a lot of hamburgers. I have ridden but three real horses; never met a real, wage-earning cowboy; attended but two college football games, one Cowboys game; and know no big-wigs."

"Perfect," I think she said.

It's all very transcendental, I suppose. You need only to dip out a thimbleful of the Pacific in order to know the ocean—if you have access to a microscope. The droplet I have lived in all my life teems with Texas organisms. Again, I'm no expert on Texas lore. I have great respect for those who have studied Sam Houston. I have not. But I grew up with Charlie Conner. In his eighty years of tilling the Texas soil, my grandfather probably knew more of the things worth knowing about this state than a warrior-politician from Tennessee whose most heralded connection with Texas soil was that he caused a lot of people to be buried in it.

My grandmother never fired a shot at anybody, but she dispatched a lot of Dominicker roosters for our Sunday dinners. She was an even better farmer than my grandfather and nourished her family with the vegetables and hens she raised, clothed us with the art of her needle, and kept us clean with the lye soap she made by the "full of the moon." She warmed our bodies with the quilts she pieced, and because of the love she stitched into them, they warmed our souls as well.

Once, when I was young and given to foolishness, I said that they never really knew very much of the good life. My Aunt Sarah Conner, ever so much wiser, gently lessoned me. "No," she said, "they had the good life all along. What the world thinks is the good life is wrong."

All of which is to say that the writing in this book proceeds from the understanding that I have gained from the contents of this cosmic thimble.

It spans the last decade of this millennium (according to popular majority). In converting radio talk to the printed page, I have made slight alterations, compressing in some places, expanding in others. At first, I tried to arrange these selections according to topic. It did not work for me, as I am incapable of writing anything that doesn't eventually seek a narrative form. The reader may see a theme emerge in 1989, maybe even a story that continues through 1999.

Generally, though, there are three topics—people and family, education, and the changes technology has wrought on the physical and social landscape of Texas.

I believe that education is the best answer to the social problems of Texas. Twenty of the selections printed here deal directly with this subject. Once upon a time, I was a teacher.

All but one of the people profiled here, thirty or more, are denizens of small towns of Texas. William Barney, from the Riverside section of Fort Worth, sees the cosmos in a tomato vine in his backyard. Two of those profiled are dogs and one is a cat. Some of my best friends have been animals, and I do not really trust people who don't like them.

Technology is an expensive friend. The alphabet expedited knowledge but lessened the importance of memory. Once, only the greatest authors made books. After moveable type, they were obliged to compete with anyone with access to a printing press, a barrel of ink, and a sordid tale to tell. Refrigerated air has cooled Texas down but swelled its population to the limit, at least if the freeways are an indication. In order to get cool, we have used freon gas, which has eaten a hole in the ozone layer. The thing that cooled us down is heating us up again. Each innovation, beginning with the fig leaf, we have paid for in the coin of human intimacy.

I feel the need to acknowledge my four fathers here. No, not my forefathers—although I am sure I owe them a great deal—but my four fathers, themselves sons of Texas. They have influenced me in ways that rival my education in importance. My grandfather, Charles Ray Conner, a farmer and railroad worker, was a gentle, unassuming, thrifty man whose imprint I will carry forever. My stepfather, Raymond Basham, if he had had the luxury of an education, could have been another Euclid. My eponymous father, Alonzo Berry Dodge, though a real man, was but a phantom to me, one I knew only in my imagination, where he was a war hero. Clarence Alonzo Mann, whom I know only through his genetic material that swells my veins, was a hell-raisin', two-fisted fightin', good-lookin' sonuvagun, and one whose resonance I have mysteriously felt all the nights and days of my life.

Tom Dodge
Midlothian, Texas
December 15, 1999

# Acknowledgements

"The School That Thrives on Sex" appeared in *Texas Monthly* as "Body Count." "Rockport's Guru of Granite," "Gainesville's Big Jungle Man," "The Coneys of No Change," and "Getting a Railroad Town Back on Track," appeared in *Texas Co-Op Power Magazine.* "Whole Wheat Nonzense" and "The Fender Skirt King of Texas" appeared in *D Magazine* in shorter form. "The Ghost of Christmas Future is Orange and Glows in the Dark," "Robert James Waller, Man or Corporation," "Topping Out on the Ground Floor," "The Warren Beatty of Dogs," and "Give Me That Old Time Mythology" appeared in the *Dallas Morning News*. The poem "Our Father Figure" was first published in *The English Journal*. "Making a Federal Case," "That Good-Tastin', Fine East Texas Muscadine Wine," "Big Splash in the Panhandle," and "Better to Reign in Hell Than Need a Car Part" are printed here for the first time. Audio versions of others aired on NPR station KERA in various different forms.

My special thanks to

Yolette Garcia, Susan Schewe, Sam Baker, Robert Wood, and Eric Bright at KERA, magicians who not only pull the rabbit out of the hat but give him a voice as well;

Jon McConal and Bryan Woolley for pointing the way to the printing press;

Ginnie Bivona, lamp of reason;

And Paul Benson, tirelessly persuading me that my garden is the best possible garden in this best of all possible worlds.

To fellow East Cleburne denizens Bill Leonard and Bill Miller. I appreciate the ready exchange of insights gained from viewing the world from the east side of the Henderson Street Bridge. And to Richard Rogers for... west-of-the-bridge ballast.

Thanks also to Julie Baker and Edward Dotson at Cleburne's Layland Museum for photos that inspired the art.

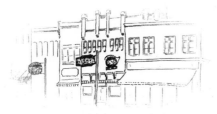

# 1989

*How easily we slipped back into our childhoods, when Vietnam was Indochina; assassination was something that happened only to presidents like Lincoln, Garfield, and McKinley; Coke was only a drink; a joint was the West Gate Café; and AIDS was a weight-loss confection.*

## Grandchildren Make You Rich

Other than receiving your official greetings from AARP, becoming a grandparent is the only American rite of passage into, uh, well, you know. This is probably why so many people have a hard time adjusting to it. It isn't easy being an overnight family patriarch. In my mind I am still the same boy in white bucks and pink sport coat who picked up that tender teenage beauty, now the grandmother, for the sock hop that started it all.

Getting older can be a pretty hairy experience if you believe the television. Commercials targeting this age group show not only the girl going off with the hirsute guy from the hair replacement factory, but they remind you that, instead of growing on your head, hair grows on your nose, on your ears, out of your ears. Your eyebrows become a veritable fount of flagella. So, after you get your toupee, you will need a depilatory. It just so happens that they have that too.

Ads show slender and muscular young people happily and sweatlessly enjoying exercise machines. Are we to believe they were old and overweight before their purchase? In any case, the television tells us to buy these contraptions. We must reduce, and dieting has no effect on anyone over forty. The only fat you lose is in your face, which is bad because the fat was the only thing holding it up. After you lose weight on the ski machine, you will need a facelift, which is also for sale.

Another shows a creaky guy getting up in the morning—without the miracle tonic. He holds his back and creeps along like a man walking into the wind. But after the tonic—he leaps out of bed like Superman.

On a late-night "infomercial" for a prostate-enhancing remedy, a former sufferer says that when he spent the night away from home, he considered connecting the bedpost to the bathroom doorknob with a string that he could follow during the night.

Unfortunately, these are our aging myths. In reality aging has more joy than travail, but in the world of television, half-truths are the coin of the realm. Joy sells no tonic.

The "upside," as baby boomers like to say, is that you have a new little pal, one like you've never had before. My little Haylee calls me "Papa," and we have lots of fun together. Almost every day there's a little voice on my recorder, saying, "Papa, would come get me when you get home?" I know what this means—and lots of quarters will be involved. We have to go down and let her ride the quarter horses in front of the grocery store. You know what quarter horses are. If not, you will soon learn. They're those little plastic carousel horses that go in a circle and eat your quarters faster than a real horse can eat oats.

Sometimes I take her down to the farm near Blum in Hill County. We have big fun down there. We sit on the wooden bridge while she drops pebbles into the creek below. She is ever so pleased to hear the plunk they make when they hit the water. My job is to see that the bucket never runs out of pebbles—good exercise without having to buy a machine.

Another bright side of patriarchy is that you no longer have to do many of the things that you were once obliged to do. "Don't bother Papa," you hear them say, "he doesn't have to go to the all-school ballerina recital if he doesn't want to." These are such sweet, wonderful words.

You no longer care very much what others think of you and are amused that they are so enslaved to public opinion and popular culture. The latest movies and even the ball scores are but dross to you. You are indifferent to fashion trends. You care only that your clothes are durable and don't bind. Your bank account swells. Has some drug dealer used your account to launder cocaine money? No, you no longer want the needless items sold in the malls, and your children are grown and have jobs of their own. That's *your* money accumulating down at the bank. Money to put into Certificates of Deposits to roll over and over and over, money to keep and love and caress.

Who would trade all this money and wisdom and felicity to be a twenty-year-old fool again?

Oh man.

· · · 🐾 · · ·

# The Return to Estelline

The Burlington Northern Special that left Fort Worth at seven A.M. last Saturday bound for Estelline carried a heavy load of quill drivers. Jane Roberts Wood had arranged for this literary express to promote her book *The Train to Estelline*. Aboard were authors like Pete Gunter, Clay Reynolds, and Mollie Ivins. There were publicists, editors, reporters, the book's publisher Ellen Templeton, as well as friends and family of the author. Just as in the novel the train stopped at Wichita Falls, Vernon, Quanah, and Childress, but this time to pick up the mayors and public officials of these towns and to allow Jane and her friend Jean Stapleton to greet the crowds and sign autographs. Ms. Stapleton is popular for her role as Edith on *All in the Family*.

People waved as the train went through the many small West Texas towns. It was the first train carrying passengers they had seen in these parts in many years, and this one carried the author of a popular book and a famous television personality.

During my brief conversation with this icon of TV culture, my Texas accent got me into trouble. She noted my guitar and said she was eager to join in the musicality that was planned for later. She said she had once studied for the opera and, in fact, would be singing in a forthcoming stage production. I said, "so, you are trained to sing." My pronunciation of "trained" sounded to her like "trying." She said,

"Oh, no! I'm not *trying* to! I'm very good at it!"

Oh, stifle.

Estelline, like many other towns in this region, is about as depressed as it can be and still stay on the map. It claims 288 souls and has a café, a city hall, a post office, an antique store, a few churches, and three liquor stores. Some find work in Childress, itself singing the unemployment blues, and others toil on the few cattle ranches that still exist in the area. Some just sit on the benches on Main Street across from the square and talk about how much better things are going to be once the new prison goes in at Childress. I asked one of the three idlers watching the literary ceremonies if he had ever seen this many people in this town. "Once," he said.

"When was that?"

"Today," he explained.

"Used to be," said one of his colleagues, "there were nearly this many people downtown every Saturday night. In those days, we had two banks, two car dealerships, five grocery stores, and a picture show."

"Is this Reagan country?"

"No, this is still Democrat country. I didn't vote for Reagan and I don't care if he knows it. I never voted for a Republican and never will, unless I lose my mind and don't know any better."

"Have you heard how many books they sold in the town?"

"Oh, a lot. They sold thirty-two over at the liquor store."

Across the street, Jane was making a speech from a flat-bed truck and thanking everyone for the reception. After this, she went to autograph books at the city hall across Highway 287.

The author's mother had come to this town in 1911 to teach school, as does the book's seventeen-year-old teacher, Lucy Richards. These townspeople are descendants of the characters in the book, and some even carry the same name. In the novel, Lucy rescues a student named Squint from a well. A real-life Squint approached the author and said, "Thanks for gittin' me outta that well."

"Your mother changed my life!" a woman told her. Another said she loved this book as much as she loved the Bible.

It was the biggest day in this town in a long time, maybe ever. Everybody turned out to meet the train and take their children on a tour through its luxurious cars. One man said this was the first passenger train most of these young people had ever seen and the most people his children had ever seen together at one time. There were cowboys, musicians, and officers of the law from

Childress—all on their best behavior for the TV news cameras. Vendors sold cactus preserves, barbecue, and books.

It was also a big day for the Burlington Northern, which bankrolled the excursion, despite the fact that the railroad was a villainous force in the novel. "That's all right, a railroad executive said. "In the book, it was the Santa Fe."

. . . 🦫 . . .

# Back Home for the Hollidays

Before the Hollidays of Cleburne moved into their new house, they had a party. They are one of the best-known and best-loved families in this town. Mr. and Mrs. Holliday—Walter and "Scooter"—opened wide the doors of their home to the boys who gathered there regularly in the 1950s to play cards. They wanted to have all of us together again one last time.

Walter, known to us all as "The Mayor" because we thought he was the only *real* mayor this town would ever have, donated the house on West Henderson Street and its property to the First Methodist Church. He is an equal-opportunity philanthropist—he gave property to other denominations, too. As mayor, he was incorruptible and sensitive to the plight of the underprivileged. Though he became successful in business, he knew he had advantages others might not have had. So he never held himself up as an example to others less successful.

The Hollidays accepted us all without regard to our address, clubs we belonged to, or grade-point average. They did this simply because we were friends of their children, Lonnie and Carol. We represented different social and economic backgrounds. Some of us were considered pestiferous by teachers; some were earnest and studious; some were star athletes. A few were even considered rowdy by local arbiters of civility. At the Holliday's, all were equal.

So we answered the call to reunite, about thirty of us, to play a few hands of cards. We are in our late forties and early fifties now. We are businessmen, lawyers, sportswriters, teachers, railroaders, dentists—all of us, I think, made good, even the pestiferous and rowdy.

Some of us are grandfathers.

We chatted awhile and then dealt the cards. Some of us hadn't played these games since we last played in this house. The ones who played hearts or gin rummy as teenagers played these games again. Those who played poker played it again—on the very same dining room table. The kibitzers of old—you guessed it—were still looking over our shoulders and whispering unwanted advice. The winners of the old days won again, and the same losers lost.

Though our experiences over the years have changed us in some ways, we remain the same in other, important ways. After one hand, someone was heard to say, "That card you played cost me the pot—and you didn't block for me in the Brownwood game either!"

How easily we slipped back into our childhoods, to that time of innocence, when Vietnam was still Indochina; assassination was something that happened only to presidents like Lincoln, Garfield, and McKinley; Coke was only a drink; a joint was the West Gate Café; and AIDS was a weight-loss confection.

There was little or no reminiscing or even catching up on one another. No one made a speech. We did what we came there to do—we played cards. There was affection among us, but it was unnecessary to state it. Such as that would take time away from the games. The old competitors still played to win. But whether we won or lost, we all knew that we were very lucky guys growing up to have been the special friends of the Hollidays.

· · · 🦃 · · ·

## Someone to Watch Over Me

Floyd Kuykendall briefly became a national figure recently when he escaped from the new county jail in Cleburne before it was officially opened for customers. When Johnson County sheriff Eddy Boggs sent Kuykendall and twenty-six other inmates over to the new facility to clean up for the big move from the old jail, Floyd lit out, along with two buddies.

They swiped a maintenance truck and, as haste makes waste, ran it into the wall of the new jail, smashing the truck's front fender. Apparently viewing this as a portent, one of these aspiring Dillingers decided that escaping wasn't all it was cracked up to be, so to speak, and forthwith broke back into the jail.

The others pushed on. They abandoned the truck and loped toward Prine's Auto Salvage on North Main where they scrunched their bodies into the trunk of a wrecked car. According to Floyd, the officers of the law came into the wrecking yard looking for him. He could hear their dogs barking and sniffing around, he thought, near the rear tires of the car.

Apparently oblivious to the dogs' sudden interest in the car, two officers stood around for what must have seemed to Floyd and his traveling companion an almost interminable time. One even put his foot on the bumper as they speculated on the various retributional procedures they would employ once they got their grabbers on these runaways. The fugitives are hearing this grisly information and concoct plans of their own. They decide, come nightfall, to put some mileage between themselves and the creative rehabilitative techniques of these irritated officers of the law.

With luck and pluck, they made it out of Cleburne. But their plans went sour. In Arlington a few days later, they pulled some more mischief and this time ran their vehicle into a tree. They were arrested and remanded to the custody of these fuming Johnson County authorities.

Floyd must have assayed his predicament with these lawmen and their plans for his homecoming and decided that his body parts might become involved. So he pulled another rich one. He wrote to the local newspaper and told his story. His life was in danger, he wrote; he had overheard these officers discussing his rehabilitation program—and it sounded like it involved pain.

This letter moved the district attorney to effect Floyd's transfer to the neighboring jailhouse in Hillsboro for safekeeping. From the relative safety of these environs, Floyd the author struck again—this time in an open letter to a weekly newspaper in Cleburne. In this missive, he vented his displeasure with the Johnson County jail, the high sheriff of that county, the guards, and the horse they rode in on.

He was miffed that they would deign to guard him, not with a regular armed lawman, but with a "construction worker." It was downright humiliating. "You can't blame me for leaving the jail that day," he goes on indignantly. "I don't know anybody who wants to stay in a jail with a sheriff who's not doing his job right."

And he doesn't care if he never sees that jail again if they're going to leave such a "dummy" in charge of him. Floyd goes on in this disgusted tone. "It's the sheriff's job to be watching me," he says, "and bringing me in when I do something bad."

Lawmen should heed Floyd's plight. Prisoners have their pride. Where do they get off using a construction worker without a real gun to guard bona fide outlaws like him?

There oughta be a law!

. . . 🐝 . . .

# Making a Federal Case

*Sleepwalking*

The prosecuting attorney in Dallas's Federal Court Building had the droopy look of Colonel Potter of the old television show, *M\*A\*S\*H*, but he lacked every appendage of that character's wit. He also made an egregiously foolish error of judgment. He apparently assumed that the law stood so unassailably against the defendant that he could sleepwalk through jury selection and through the trial itself. He further erred by sharing the prosecution table with a deputy federal marshal whose severe, pitiless features came to symbolize for most members of the jury every fear they ever had about the police.

At the defense table sat the marshal's antithesis, one Theodore Miller, charged with "knowingly and willingly absenting himself from the custody of the Attorney General." In other words, our Theodore was said to have escaped from the federal penitentiary at Seagoville, a few miles southeast of Dallas.

During preliminary jury selection that morning he wore spacious prison grays and looked like a lost, desperate spaniel, searching the room for a friend. His two court-appointed attorneys seemed as if they weren't sure whether they had shown up for the right trial. They were spectacularly mediocre, yet they managed to seat eight jurors who would vote with their client on the first ballot.

Presiding was Judge Robert Hill, regal and majestic in his black robes. He peered down in such a way at the defense table that some members of the jury would come to suspect that his honor did not exactly have his life's savings invested in the future of Theodore Miller.

### Miller's Dozen

In answer to one of the perfunctory questions during jury selection—whether anyone has ever filed a lawsuit against the federal government—a hefty woman rose and said, her voice quaking with fear, "My husband and I have a suit against Montgomery Ward's."

For a moment, it looked as though his honor might blow his solemnity sky high. He banged his gavel to quell the laughter that this meek, misguided woman had unintentionally detonated by her valiant attempt to place as many miles as possible between herself and this case. His honor's Adam's apple bobbed as he fought to swallow his laughter. He gazed at her over his glasses and said softly:

"Madam, Montgomery Ward's is a department store. It is not affiliated with the federal government."

Even our Ted, who, up until this time, had seemed hopelessly grim, grinned at this absurd turn of the courtroom mood as if he knew it had shifted in his favor. Until this moment, the tide of justice had been flowing steadily out, carrying his fate with it. But there was a new mood in the courtroom, and in keeping with it, his lawyers chose this unwitting detonator of laughter as the first juror, determined to go with this new flow wherever it took them.

The next juror selected was a woman who worked as a cook. The others included a drug rehabilitation center director, an

Amway saleslady, a young commercial artist, a small-engine repairman, a sphinx-like woman whose father was a police officer, a legal secretary, two women identifying themselves as "housewives," a computer salesman, and a college professor. Seven women and five men. One, like the defendant, black.

### Open and Shut

Theodore Miller, decked out for the trial in a suit that looked as if it were also court-appointed, rose at the judge's order and stated his answer to the charge against him: "Not guilty."

Colonel Potter sleepily outlined what the government intended to prove. His body language proved, however, that what he really wanted was a nap.

The defense countered with an assertion that on the weekend in question the defendant was awarded a furlough to go home and settle some family business. There were over a dozen witnesses to testify that the defendant's brother-in-law had made "terroristic threats" against the defendant's wife and mother-in-law. These witnesses would further testify to the uprightness of the defendant's character and his devotion to his family—exemplified by four previous furloughs, which he had honored each time by his prompt return.

This time, however, when he was preparing to return with the usual promptness, the brother-in-law showed up in the household making his terroristic threats. The police were called but left after declaring it a "family squabble." Desperate, as the sole defender of the family, Theodore called the prison for instructions. A functionary told him that an extension was out of the question and to get back there by five. Our Theodore then called his probation officer, who told him that only a warden can extend a furlough and that it was impossible to contact him on a Sunday. Witnesses would substantiate all this.

Colonel Potter roused himself to semiconsciousness and called the government's witnesses. They testified that old Theodore had by god escaped from the Seagoville pen and there were no two ways about it. The Texas Department of Corrections functionary who issued the furlough testified that Theodore Miller signed a document requiring him to be back on Sunday at five and that five came and no Theodore. Yes, the defendant had called and asked for an extension but was told to haul it on back.

The deputy marshal, he of the menacing features, then took the stand and stated that he and his partner had been dispatched to the defendant's residence nine days after his leavetaking, that they entered through a back window after attempts to raise anyone failed and found the defendant hiding in a closet. Hearing this, our Theodore commenced shaking his head in a dramatic show of protest that this officer would perpetrate such a foul slander against his manhood.

About all the defense could elicit from the witness to ameliorate the damage was a substitution of "standing" for "hiding."

The defense called one of the police officers who had been summoned to the Miller household fracas. He was summarizing his account when the judge interrupted with a question that significantly lowered the value in that courtroom of Theodore Miller Stocks and Commodities. "Was the defendant injured in any way?" the judge asked, his voice as dry as July hay. "Was he able to walk?"

No, he was not injured. Yes, he could walk.

What the judge said next sent the case to the jury: "The witness has testified that the defendant was uninjured and able to walk; therefore was physically able to return to his place of incarceration by the appointed time. So I'm going to disallow further testimony from the witness and from subsequent defense witnesses unless they can testify to the physical disability of the defendant to return."

That was it. The neatness and clarity of the statement and the effortlessness of its presentation lent credence to the possibility that his honor had practiced it in front of the mirror the night before. After a brief discussion at the bench, both sides rested.

The judge read his charge to the jury, a detailed explanation of the law and its application to this case, then announced that he had an important engagement at four o'clock. If there was no verdict by then, the jury would have to return the next day.

*To establish specific intent the government must prove that the defendant knowingly did an act which the law forbids, purposely intending to violate the law.*

from Judge Hill's charge to the jury

The computer salesman opened deliberation proceedings with the recommendation that the professor serve as foreman. The professor declined and recommended the Amway representative. She accepted and proceeding continued.

Amway: "I would like to have a vote now to see if everybody might accidentally be in agreement. Does anybody have anything to say first?"

Computer salesman: "I think the man was just defending his home and family, and it's a sad day when a man is not allowed to do that."

Legal secretary: "It's not a matter of him not being allowed to do that. It's a matter of him escaping from prison. He was supposed to return to the prison and he didn't. It's as simple as that."

Cook: "Are we allowed to show some compassion here?"

L.S. "We're required to be dispassionate and objective."

Cook: "Well, I can't help it. I know when the laws came after my boy, he ran and hid under the house because he was scared.

They just drug him out and took him to jail. And they looked just like that scary policeman out there in the court."

The professor, who had been studying the furlough signed by the defendant: "This document states that Miller was to 'remain within the limits of his extended confinement.' Doesn't that mean his residence? Wasn't he there when they came and got him?"

L.S.: "Yes—nine days late."

Amway: "Well, I'm not so sure you can blame him. Who else was going to protect his family if he didn't? Certainly not the police. He's a convict with no civil rights. What are the police going to do for him?"

L.S.: "I didn't say I blamed him. I would probably have done the same thing—but I would have been prepared to pay the consequences for not obeying the law."

A vote of eight to four was taken, in favor of the defendant.

Professor: "I don't think he was necessarily able to return on time. There's no question that he was physically able, but what about mentally? His family was in danger. His lawyers should have brought this up."

Several jurors at once, laughing: "They didn't bring up much of anything!"

L.S.: "Evidently, mental inability is not a legal defense. At least we were not told to consider it."

Amway: "Anyone else before we vote again?"

Computer: "We can vote till Kingdom Come and I'll vote not guilty every time."

The vote this time was ten not guilty, two guilty.

Commercial artist: "I changed my vote because they should have taken his mental condition into consideration."

Small engine repairman: "I changed mine, too, for the same reason."

L.S.: "That's not a legal reason for changing your vote. The stipulation was physical ability only."

Montgomery Ward's: "Well, he's already in prison. What do they want to do—sentence him to life on the street?"

Professor: "I've been studying this furlough again. The key word is "knowingly." Remember, in the judge's charge, he said Miller knowingly absented himself from the custody of the Attorney General? Not a single witness testified that Miller knew he would be considered escaped if he remained, as it says here in this furlough, 'within the limits of his extended confinement.' Maybe he had no idea he was considered escaped as long as he was in his own home. No one told him differently. Plus, we don't know if he can even read or not. No one testified that he could. He obviously knew that he was late, because he called and asked for an extension. But no one testified that he was told he would be considered escaped if he didn't get back on time. 'Escaped' in his mind is probably no different from what it is in ours—that you tunnel out or get a gun and shoot your way out. It's possible that he thought he was fulfilling the agreement in the furlough by doing what it said—'remaining within the limits of his extended confinement.' I might have thought the same thing myself because of the ambiguous way it's written."

Computer: "That's right! If the man was going to escape, do you think he would be hanging around his own place? Nobody escapes from the pen and hangs around his own house. That's ridiculous."

Amway: "And I'm wondering—if they were so worried about him being escaped, why did they wait nine days before they finally got around to going out and looking for him? The whole thing is screwy."

Another vote came out eleven not guilty, one guilty.

L.S.: "I changed my vote because of what *he* said," pointing to the professor. "The possibility that he didn't know he was escaped bothered me enough that I changed my vote. Probably he did know it. But there's still that doubt. And that's all it takes to acquit—a reasonable doubt."

Rehab: "I guess I'm the only hold-out. But I still think we're forgetting the basic issue here—he went on furlough; he didn't come back and was placed on escaped status. To me it's as simple as that. I think we're mincing words, but I'm willing to go along rather than hang the jury."

Computer: "That's it! Not guilty!"

### Shocked

When Amway stood and stated the verdict of not guilty, the judge was visibly astounded. His face ashened as the weight of what he had heard reached the overload mechanism in his brain that triggers the shock alarm. His lower lip quivered slightly and his jaw dropped. He riveted a glare at the defendant, who had leaped to his feet in joy and was waving at the jury. "SIT DOWN OVER THERE!" his honor suggested.

Our Theodore quickly and dutifully took the hint.

Colonel Potter roused himself from his torpor and gazed quizzically at the marshal, who grimaced and bared his teeth.

The defense attorneys were so stunned that they seemed to be on the verge of asking for a retrial.

The judge gathered his composure, thanked the jury menacingly, and excused it from further service.

By the time the jury members arrived at the deliberation room to collect their things, his honor was there. "Was something wrong?" he said, still ashen. "The verdict didn't go as we had expected."

"The furlough document was, uh, vague," said Amway, "and made us have a reasonable doubt."

"I'll take a look at it," he said. "It may have to be rewritten. Someone may contact you about that. You were fooled by him, by the way," he added. "He's a very good actor. And he's escaped before. But we couldn't tell you that."

Some of the jury members sighed audibly. L.S. said, "Oh, no!"

His honor continued to turn the thumbscrews. "He's been in trouble of one kind or another since he was seventeen. He's serving a seven-year sentence now. I gave it to him."

Some of the jury members rode the same shuttle bus back to the parking lot at Reunion Arena. Amway turned to L.S. and said, "Do you regret your vote?"

"No," she said. She pointed to the professor sitting on the other side of the bus. "I regret that he put that doubt in my mind."

. . . ❦ . . .

## For Boys, It's Girls Over Ethics Every Time

As an experiment, Joshua voters elected a high school senior to the school board. Larry Marlar was studious, polite, and ambitious—a real go-getter. Three weeks later he used his position to go and get the physics exam and give it to his girlfriend.

At a special school board meeting where he admitted his guilt, he was publicly censured by the other members and asked to resign.

He wouldn't resign, but he said he was sorry for what he did and would atone if given the chance. A Cleburne newspaper article added a twist to the story: The student had campaigned in support of the high school principal, whose contract had not been renewed by the board. The story goes on to say that the principal did not report the incident to the boy's parents or to the superintendent's office. The newspaper quotes the principal as telling the physics teacher that "this is as far as it should go."

In a letter to the editor of the same newspaper, a classmate severely reprimanded the young board member for his moral lapse. He was too immature, she wrote, to represent the school as a trustee, and his behavior would unfairly brand the school as one of "cheating and dishonesty." She called for stronger punishment than censure.

This bizarre story put Joshua into the news briefly, bringing, as the letter writer said, more bad publicity than good. However, I don't think the public will judge an entire school by one student's misbehavior, or even the student, for that matter. Adolescence is not the period known for wisdom. The question is, will he atone?

People are interested in the story because it shows two things. It is a lesson in public and private morality, in other words, appearances versus reality. He was a student with all the apparent morality that a small town could hope for in a young man. But his behavior came as a surprise to those who rely only on appearances. There are, I am convinced, students in that school with only C averages, wearing clothes with the wrong labels, belonging to the wrong clubs, having the wrong addresses, who could have served in that office honestly and capably.

The story also carries the implication that boys are likely to wager purgatory for the favor of a girl. It is a compelling story, the oldest and most universal of all themes. It is the biblical story of a man, a woman, and forbidden fruit. To please her, he will just about always bite the apple.

In another familiar Bible story, Delilah uses her charms on Samson to get the answer to his riddle.

In a Greek story, Paris chooses Aphrodite as the fairest of the goddesses because she bribes him with the favors of the most beautiful woman in the world.

And these storied examples were adults, adults with heaven's blessings. Men can be fools at any age, but at eighteen, testosterone rules. An old man deserves no credit for his sexual rectitude, as Mark Twain says, and should withhold his condemnation of these youthful lapses. Return to him his youth and he will ruin the first young girl to cross his path.

This is because girls generally come first with boys. Then, when they grow up, these boys might become John Tower and Wilbur Mills and Wayne Hayes and Dwight Eisenhower and John Kennedy and Gary Hart, all capable legislators and leaders, all patriotic and God-fearing. But all of them still boys, willing to risk everything for careless love.

There may be one more lesson to be found in this story—if Joshua voters still want a student on the school board, then they should consider the possibility that the best boy for the job might just be a girl.

· · · ❦ · · ·

## The School That Thrives on Sex

J.J. Barlow, the sly old dog of a superintendent of the Patton Springs Independent School District, isn't interested in hiring geniuses to teach at the school in Afton. He wouldn't want Nobel Prize winners if they were celibate. He would much rather hire an ordinary teacher with an extraordinary libido. "Let's put it this way," he says, pushing back a shock of graying hair from his brow. "We don't recruit, but if we were looking for a teacher and we had a qualified applicant with eight children, that teacher would be likable right off the bat." He resembles Will Rogers as he squints at you and grins in a rural-friendly way.

To Barlow, nothing is more important than having ninety students in his school district. Fewer means significantly less funding, fewer teachers and educational programs. Drop to a number very much lower than that and there is no school at all. In small, impoverished school districts like Afton's the major source of funding is state money. The state provides about half the cost of educating students; most of the rest comes from local property taxes. Districts with large tax bases supplement the state dole with ease, but for a poor district, the only hope is to receive as much state money as possible. To do so, the district must keep its enrollment above ninety, an important number in the state's method of determining funding. If a district has fewer students than that, the state pays $1,477 per student yearly. But a district with more than ninety students receives much more, as if it had 130 students.

For Afton's Patton Springs school this year, with 102 students (seventy percent Anglo, thirty percent Mexican-American) kindergarten through twelfth grade, losing an employee with several children could be devastating. When five people resigned at the end of the school year, the enrollment suddenly dropped by eighteen. "It got dangerously close to that ninety mark," Barlow says.

With so much state money on the line, any superintendent would prefer an applicant who had been more prolific in the bedroom than in the classroom, one who had written the book of love rather than the great American novel. Ever enterprising, Barlow last year hired new personnel with a total of sixteen children.

Asked about this hiring coup, he grins as if he had just sold aluminum siding to a man with a brick house. He says, "It's no different from these bigger schools. When they're hiring a basketball coach, they give the edge to an applicant who has a six-five son. That's just the way it goes."

How can such a poor West Texas school district ever hope to attract teachers, with or without children? The nearest shopping mall is in Lubbock, seventy miles to the west; and you have to go three miles just to get to Cooper's Grocery, the only "convenience" store. Its terrain is rugged and its weather harsh; occasionally, for excitement, you might see a roadrunner swallowing a whipsnake. The wind blows so hard sometimes the lightning can't strike. Other than the school, the only architecture in Afton is a post office and a cotton gin. The school is the only industry for the entire population—forty or fifty, depending on your source. It was built in 1935 and is unchanged except for the addition of tinted windows and water coolers. Forming a semicircle around it are the "teacherages," modest homes for the teachers who live there free of charge, no rent, no utilities. The largest is where the superintendent lives. The next largest, across Farm Road 193, is the principal's, and so on down the line. "They're cozy but not as modern as the ones in Guthrie," says Barlow, referring to a district forty miles away that has a tax base of $260 million, as opposed to Afton's $22 million.

Given Afton's circumstances, it isn't surprising that many of its teachers are just passing through—young teachers getting a start, old administrators on their way to retirement. But one who intends to stay is Leonard Stan, a sixty-two-year-old first generation American from the Bronx who teaches science and math. Stan (his father shortened it from Stankevitch when he emigrated from Russia) has lived in one of the teacherages since 1983 and has put down roots as deep as those of the mesquite trees that he burns in his stove. He left New York in 1958 to play minor league baseball, ending up with the old Dallas Rangers. After the team disbanded, he got a master's degree from North Texas State College. Along the way he married a classmate, a philosophy major from Matador. They taught in Dallas, had two children, Jonah and Cassandra, relocated to New Mexico, divorced. He moved to Afton to forget. Now that he has forgotten, he says, he will stay.

He likes people; he just doesn't like them in malls and traffic jams. His socializing now involves chaperoning the senior trips to places like Mexico City and the Bahamas, his way paid by money they raise. During the school year he accompanies the school's six-man football teams on their out-of-town games, sometimes as far away as 250 miles. Every day after school he rides his bike along the lonely blue highways and swims all year round in the ice-cold, spring-fed pool at Roaring Springs Ranch club, five miles away. He missed swimming only once, when ice prevented his getting to the ranch.

During the growing season he lives off the vegetables, free to the public, from the community garden tended by the agriculture class. He shops at Sam's Wholesale Club in Lubbock twice a month for industrial-sized containers of cereal, grains, olive oil, and whole-wheat bread. He attributes his perfect health to this regimen, and to the massive amounts of garlic he eats from the garden. His students call him "Stan, Stan, the garlic man."

Superintendent Barlow admits that not all teachers are so satisfied with life in Afton. They prefer Guthrie, of course, with its 6666 Ranch money and higher salaries, fancier teacherages, and local stores. Nearby Sudan (398 students) is also more prosperous, with its $607 million tax base due to the power plant located there.

"People move out here initially," Barlow says, "because it's the only place they can afford to live." There are scores of abandoned farmhouses in the Motley County area, available to anyone willing to fix them up and pay the taxes on them. "There's no drug problem," he goes on, "no crime. We leave the gym open all the time, and no one ever steals the equipment. They know if they do, we'll close it up. About the worst thing that happens around here is that a boy will drive onto the football field or tennis court and do doughnuts."

Afton may be a backwater, but it has students who respect the school. "They've been taught by their parents," Barlow goes on, "that it represents the only way out—there are no jobs other than at the school. There are only two kinds of people here—the rich and the poor, and the rich have jobs."

Enrollment is good now, so the Patton Springs school is secure for at least one more year. As Barlow nears retirement, he looks forward to moving to his farm near Earth, 112 miles to the west. There, he will look after his ninety-five-year-old mother and start a legume business, which he will call Earth Foods for Earth People. He has noted the comparison between the two occupations, but as a bean farmer he will need be concerned only with the fertility of his fields.

As for Lennie Stan, happiness is teaching math to his half-dozen students, biking new trails, and raising a good garlic crop at the community garden.

# The Tiger Jones of Footwear

In the old days, Cleburne had two shoe repair shops, one of them neat and orderly with modern equipment, and the other owned and operated by Raymon (Doc) McDearmon. Doc was a serious Yellow Jackets fan, and so his shop became a gathering place for team members from as far back as the 1941 team and their friends. They grew up but never got too far away from the shoe shop. They were an assortment of faded heroes whose deeds on the field had long since been replaced in the town's consciousness by other younger warriors, and the old heroes' exploits were forgotten everywhere but inside Doc's shop. He had thumbtacked their winning catches and jolting tackles to the walls in a gallery of seasons past, a tribute to youth's dreams outworn.

Then, there was myself, from the class of '57, high school sportswriter and admirer of these erstwhile touchdownsmen. I didn't mind that their lives had peaked at eighteen and that subsequent years had brought a significant downturn in their fortunes, and neither did Doc. The Korean War set them back and they never recovered, Doc told me. A few of them worked at the railroad, and some were day laborers. But mainly they seemed to be permanently "between jobs." One of these was Ralph Junell, class of '48 and unofficial leader of the shoe shop gang. He had been a star with college prospects, but a back injury had ended his play. Other than the fact that he was known as the Rocky Marciano of Cleburne and the south side of Fort Worth, I knew little else about him. Once, I asked a member of his circle about the true nature of Ralph's livelihood and was told that he was a "jeweler." (No one would ever ask Ralph such a question. In fact, he did not entertain conversation from anyone outside his elite circle of associates.)

Actually, Doc told me, Ralph was currently the bodyguard for the pretty widow of a Fort Worth mob boss whose body had recently been extracted from a Godley surface well. She gave our hero a steady trove of diamonds as tokens of her precious, devoted love, and he had hocked them just as steadily and devotedly.

His associates were equally adept at acquiring funds. Mostly, they were gamblers. They met at Doc's and learned where the games were that day. On Mondays they went to Fort Worth for free beer. They always seemed to know where the beer supplier was giving out samples.

Doc wasn't a gambler or a drinker. He had perfect attendance down at the Church of Christ. His honesty had no limits. If a customer brought in a pair of cheap shoes for repair, he would say, "Not worth it. Go buy a new pair."

That they just went down the street to the other shop bothered him not at all. "Gotta sleep at night," he said.

Some people wondered why Doc allowed the boys to hang out there. Their reputations didn't exactly carry the Chamber of Commerce seal of approval. Doc picked up a pair of boots from his workbench. "See these boots?" he said. "Number-three grade leather. Not much better than pasteboard. "See these?" He picked up another pair. "Hand-tooled leather, tanned from packerhides, anilined-dyed. Number-one grade. They look the same from a distance, but when you look close you see the difference. These boys have their ways of making a living—they're not my ways—but I think they're number-one grade. I know a lot of shined-up number-three grade people, but you don't have to look too deep to see the pasteboard."

From behind his unimaginably cluttered workbench piled high with tools, boxes of tacks and bootnails, cans of hotpot glue, shoes and boots in various states of repair, Doc chatted about sports as he sewed, hammered, and carved new life back into old leather. His favorite boxer was middleweight Tiger Jones. "He's beat all of them at one time or another," he said, "but never for the title. He won't go along with the garlic boys, so he'll never get the big action. I wish I could tell him how much better he is than all the rest."

Doc is dust now, but when I drive by the spot where his shoe shop used to be, I think about him and his theories of people and leather and Tiger Jones.

I wish I had told him how much better I think he was than all the rest.

· · · 🍇 · · ·

# That Good-Tastin', Fine East Texas Muscadine Wine

The only commercial Muscadine vineyard in Texas is owned and tended by Malcolm Davis and his brother, Lane, a couple of slow-talkin' good old boys from Emory, in Rains County. They call it Martins Mill Vineyard, twelve acres of sandy land that produce a hundred tons of grapes a year. It is located two miles north of the Martins Mill school and six miles east of Canton.

Malcolm is a robust and friendly mathematical maven who talks in quantum theories and walks in quadratic equations. His white hair and blue Celtic eyes make you think of clouds and sky. He has a broad rural forehead and a quick, sanguine nose that is Bacchus-blessed: a nose that can correctly sniff out the aroma of his several different species of fruit, including Summit and Sugargate.

He got his degree from the University of Texas in Aeronautical Engineering in 1960, a helluva lot of light-years away from the one-room school at Emory. He has honor society plaques, backgammon trophies, and Outstanding Young Man awards. He also has a silver medal, won in the 1985 Lone Star Wine Competition for his Chateaux Texas wine.

On the surface, he might seem an unlikely pioneer, with his north Dallas office in Preston Center, his Mercedes-Benz, and his actuary license. Underneath, though, he is the sandy-land plowboy whose ties to East Texas run a lot deeper than to Preston Center. In Monte Carlo or Istanbul for backgammon tournaments, he operates on the edges of mystery, but there's nothing mysterious about where he looks for cherished values. For these, he turns to the likes of neighbor Winford Sides, a hardy, leguminous man of modest proportions, the official "Black-Eyed Pea King of Texas"; and to Ronnie Dawson, the Ellis County troubadour, a long, tall Texan whose musical poetry celebrates the better values of their rural upbringings.

There is a kind of "Harvest Home" party going on at the Martins Mill Vineyard and I am invited. The winding dirt road leading to it is shaded from the oppressive August sun by a canopy of elm and sweet gum. Winford's thirty-acre pea patch, which he harvests, along with hundreds of others spread over three counties, lies adjacent to the vineyard. It must wait a few more days before harvesting.

The vineyard comprises thirty rows of Muscadine vines, a quarter of a mile long and twelve feet wide, full and green with decorative interlacings of copiously appointed hanging ornaments. They stretch toward the southwest like graduating soldiers in parade dress. The drought of 1978 ruined the brothers' first crop, so that's when they put in the deep well that now provides twenty-five gallons of sweet aquifer water a day for each of the 2,000 plants.

We are all gathered in the well house—Ronnie, who has brought his guitar for his own brand of picking; his mother Gladys; Lennie Stan, bouncer at the Levee from the old days and nights when Ronnie was the headliner at that Mockingbird Avenue club; Winford; a couple of Malcolm's backgammon buddies; and some neighbor ladies who routinely help with the picking. A southern breeze, which has found its way through the open windows, is also, thankfully, in attendance.

By way of answering my questions, Malcolm explains the mathematical precision with which the vineyard is designed: "The posts are hand-located and uniformly set at three-foot depths, the hole in each post parallel to the ground and perpendicular to the rows so that the special cross-arms that hold the fifteen miles of nine-gauge galvanized steel wires that support the trellis system could be bolted to the posts. The end posts," he goes on, "which must support their share of twelve to fifteen tons of grapes per row, are specially selected steel drain pipe set five-feet deep in concrete." Some other things, I forget what, exactly, "are set precisely within a margin of one-sixteenth of an inch. It's called the 'Geneva Double Curtain' and is the absolute best for maximum yield." And so on.

Ronnie leans over to me and whispers: "Malcolm thinks it's arithmetic that makes his wine so good. But most of it's because his good vibes get into the grapes."

We sling canvas bags over our shoulders and plunge into the ranks of green. After unloading each bag, all meet back at the well house for a drink. We all admit that we ate almost as many as we brought back.

In the well house for lunch, Malcolm serves Winford's speckled butterpeas, oat bran skillet pone, and wine from the vineyard.

Ronnie straps on his guitar afterwards and asks Winford to name his favorite tune. Winford knows everything there is to know about peas but can't come up with a single song title. So Ronnie cuts down on "Silver Thread and Golden Needles," and Winford says, "That's it!"

It is a festive, Homeric concert as sweet as Muscadine wine:

*There was none but delight in the banquet*
*Before them, nor in the gorgeous lyre that Apollo*
*Played, nor yet in the dulcet Muses, who*
*Entertained them in harmonious song.*

As for me, I hardly know one wine from another but suspect that Chateaux Texas, 1988 vintage, will be a favorite if, as Ronnie says, "good vibes and feelin's" have anything to do with it.

# 1990

*As a college teacher, I labored for twenty-six years to encourage young high school graduates to think for themselves. It was the hardest part of my job.*

## Love Versus Oedipus Wrecks

My next-door neighbor hasn't seen *Field of Dreams* or read *Iron John*, Robert Bly's book on solving the mysteries of father-son relationships. He has never attended a workshop or seminar on "parenting." These currently popular activities played no role in his decision to use a wrecked pickup as a project to teach responsibility as well as enjoy some extra closeness with his teenaged son.

Ken Barker knew that Chad, fifteen, would be driving soon, but just going down to the car lot and buying him a car was not quite right. "Just look at that parking lot," he told me, pointing to the Midlothian High School parking lot across the way from our backyards. "You see all these new cars and pickups, and you know these kids can't possibly appreciate them." He said that one kid he knows burned his engine up, not once, but three times, simply because he didn't want to take the time to check the oil.

So when the time came, Ken bought his brother's 1983 Chevrolet pickup. Its paint was shot and the interior worn, he said, but it had a sound engine and straight body. So they began their restoration project in their garage, dad and son, side by side, every afternoon and evening, sometimes till midnight. They re-covered the seats and replaced the headliner. They stripped off the old paint, removed the dents, and sanded the body smooth. They applied a coat of primer and painted the truck black. They shined up the chrome and put on new tires and wheels. A minor tune-up came last, and the truck was ready to roll.

All this took several months to complete. Then, there were several more months before Chad would be old enough to get his license.

But the time eventually passed, and Chad was legal. He drove the truck proudly around town for a year or more. He appeared to be an unusually safe driver, but one day he hit a curve on a rain-slick street near his house and went into a tree, mangling a fender, wiping out the under-carriage, and twisting the frame.

"There's no other way to tell you this, Dad," he said on the telephone. "I wrecked the truck, and you have to come and get me."

The only thing Ken said was, "Are you hurt? Is anyone else hurt?" That was all. No yelling. No humiliating lectures. No sarcasm. "Why do that to him?" Ken said. "He was harder on himself than anyone else could have ever been on him. He thought his life was ruined. In fact, I had to push him back behind the wheel again."

After that, phase-two of the Barker father-son program began. They went to a wrecking yard, got a fender and a front-end, and began work. The work has been going on now for several months. Chad learned so much during the original project, his dad said, that he can do much of the work himself now. I see him every afternoon, sanding, painting, bolting on body parts. The only thing they had to hire out was straightening the frame. This has been a hold-up, but Chad has learned patience, a hard lesson for a teenager. From working on the earlier project, he learned also the necessity of doing things methodically and in their proper order. He knows the truck will be on the road soon.

Inside the garage, also, is the shell of a Volkswagen Beetle convertible. It has been freshly painted a pastel color but has no top or seats yet. I asked about it. Ken smiled. "We have teenaged daughters, too," he said.

· · · 🐝 · · ·

## Mind Who You Shun: They Might Get Famous

A former student called the other day to tell me that she was a journalist now and working on her first story for a real paper. Vicki Smith's story was on Stevie Ray Vaughn, the blues musician who had recently died in a helicopter crash.

Her angle was that he had been a kid from her Oak Cliff neighborhood in Dallas and that they had attended the same school until he dropped out. There had been little that was memorable about him, she said, and he quickly skipped out of her memory. Then several years later, she was in a record store in California and saw his picture on an album cover! He was famous!

"I can't say this in my story," she went on, "but he was considered, well, a nobody, in school, and none of us had anything to do with him. He was just the skinny kid who spent all his time playing his guitar instead of studying."

She told me of how badly the popular kids treated him and how the drill team girls, including her, ignored him. How the teachers saw him as just another faceless kid who was there in presence only and who would never amount to anything. She wished she could say these things in her story.

"That *is* your story," I told her. I encouraged her to write it just as she had told it to me. I don't know whether she did or not, but it's a story that can't be told too many times. It may be too hard for her to admit some of these things about herself in print, but I tried to explain to her that she was but a child then, and children only mirror the values of adults. It is the teachers and principals, parents, ministers, and other figures of authority who should feel the shame. They should know by their experience that many successful people were rejected as youths and should teach this to young people.

Many others, of course, turn out badly. So it is easy to justify this condemnatory rationale. See there, it is said, they really weren't worth it after all, and it's a good thing we didn't waste time on them.

Most of these shunned youngsters with talent lack Stevie Ray's drive to succeed. He may have used his rejection as motivation. We can all think of famous artists, of all fields, unappreciated by teachers and the like, but who were invited back as celebrities to the very schools that had rejected them. This kind of belated affection is also commonplace among town leaders, especially when there's a chance to cash in. Janis Joplin was virtually run out of Port Arthur, but now the city leaders have erected a monument to her on public property. Elvis Presley wasn't a member of the Junior Chamber of Commerce in his home town of Tupelo, Mississippi, and you won't find his picture in the "Most Popular" section of the high school yearbook either. Yet that town now profits from the exploitation of his fame.

Schools and towns will continue to ignore the "misfits" and concentrate all their attention on the little bright-eyed "boosters," a term coined by another famous outcast, Sinclair Lewis.

The ball players and drill team cuties will keep on shunning the Stevie Rays and Elvises and Janices, and my student's first story won't do much to change that.

But it has certainly changed *her*.

• • • ❦ • • •

# Big Splash in the Panhandle

July came to the tiny Panhandle town of Canadian with a blaze of searing heat and a warning of "winter eternal." The West Texas sun and a cloudless sky provided the heat. The warning came from the muted cry of a gigantic bronzed figure called *Forerunner*, the latest sculpture from the hand of Dallas artist William Pochciol.

"*Forerunner* has no identity beyond his message," Pochciol tells the 350 invited guests who have come for the unveiling. The setting is "The Citadel," a lavishly renovated former Baptist church and town centerpiece belonging to Dr. and Mrs. Malouf Abraham, who are hosting this event. "He is the harbinger of chaos," the artist goes on, "the coming of winter eternal. I hope his message doesn't come true." Pochciol is a robust classicist with tight blond curls and a romantic social consciousness.

An "environment in turmoil" is the theme of this gathering of mostly oil-and-gas-rich Texans, who traversed the long blue highways of West Texas to get here. The street adjacent to the spectacle is cordoned off by police. It is lined with Mercedes-Benzes and other expensive cars, and the school parking lot across the street looks like a Cadillac dealership.

Dallas book tycoon and environmentalist Ken Gjemre, founder of Half-Price Books, gives the dedicatory address. "This young artist in the tradition of Rodin is telling us we are going to have to save this earth and the species that live upon it," he says.

A soloist with the Santa Fe Opera, Joe Bolin, sings "The Star Spangled Banner"—both verses.

Abraham, forty-eight, a physician in Canadian, spent $100,000 just for the setting of this newest acquisition. Doing this included buying the house next door because it was located on the spot where he wanted the sculpture to stand. "For such a great work, every teenie thing had to be just right," he says.

He also bought the house on the other side because he wanted its alleyway. "You buy the neighborhood," this Panhandle Gatsby tells the crowd, "and zone it the way you want it." Actually, he is joking, he says. In fact, the town is so depressed that people often call him up and ask him to buy their houses.

Though he usually turns them down, such a transaction could be arranged, whether they like it or not, if they happen not to share his taste in art. Referring to his squabble with neighbors about the monument, he adds: "Anybody who doesn't like the naked statue, we'll buy their house and give them ten days to get out."

The Abrahams are among Texas' nost noted ethnic pioneers. Malouf's grandfather came from Lebanon in 1913 and settled in Canadian, where Malouf's father was born. The senior Abraham was a shrewd businessman and invested heavily in oil and gas rights. Though the bust has "dented" the family fortune, cutting their income in half, "we haven't let it get us down," Abraham says. They still donate to local charities, such as the Abraham Nursing Home in Canadian and the local YMCA.

At dusk, on the brilliant green lawn, guests graze on the gormands of the west. A woman with a system of pulchritude that would make a centerfold girl look like a cook on a sludge barge watches as her boyfriend, David Niven's grandson, films the event.

Another, in billowing muslin and leaving behind her a fragrance of money, glides among the grandees with her own special kind of Swiss movement.

The sculptor's ebullient wife, Molly, herself a classical pianist, hovers, always nearby. She is a charming but formidable protector. "When I was five," she tells the audience, I wanted to marry Beethoven when I grew up. But, when I was twenty-nine, I met Rodin."

They met in 1981 in Waxahachie where Pochciol shared a studio in a tombstone mill with Jesùs Bautista Moroles, now one of the leading granite sculptors in the country. Molly came to look at Pochciol's art and ended up with the artist. He and Moroles earned paychecks between infrequent sales by carving and setting tombstones. Pochciol's only big sale back then was an eighteen by twenty-four-foot wood carving, now hanging in the student center at Texas A&M's Maritime University at Galveston. The $15,000 this commission brought was spent long before it was finished. He often worked twenty hours a day to keep his mind off hunger. He knew he had hit bottom, he says, when the town drunk bought his breakfast.

His sensibilities still center on the same socially conscious, blue-collar work ethic he learned from his parents growing up in Pittsburgh, where he was born in 1943. His commission from *Forerunner* won't change anything, he says, except, maybe, to allow him to move Molly and their young daughter, Isis, out of their small house in east Dallas.

Inside The Citadel, in its twenty-five-hundred square-foot living room—once the church sanctuary—with its twenty-two-foot ceiling, antiques, paintings and *objet d'art*, Amarillo's Timothy

Jenkins, one of the Metropolitan Opera's promising stars, sings Strauss's "Befreit." His soaring notes ionize the evening air like desert lightning.

Out in the courtyard, frozen in his opulent surroundings, *Forerunner* lurches forever forward, like a frightened Hercules.

· · · ❦ · · ·

# Give 'em Hell, Harry

That fall semester I scanned the new students, wondering, as usual, which of them would still be there after the drop date and, of these, which would join the statistical few who actually graduate. As the eye naturally searches for the uncommon, mine quickly settled on a bearded, burly guy in a short-sleeved shirt, with tattoos covering his massive forearms. Those arms seemed to need desks of their own.

Harry Enckhausen was a very scary guy. Well, he could be, when he tried. He had a withering glare when displeased. When he talked, his classmates looked as if they wanted to get under their desks in the civil defense position. When these vocal chords from hell resonated, the chalk seemed to rattle in the trays. Most of the time, though, he just tried to fit in with the little unwrinkled peas rolling along the educational conveyer belt. After a semester or two, he established himself as an honor student and advisor to younger classmates. They learned quickly not to trash the professor, ask for test answers, or copy his homework. Any student foolish enough to ask him who was an "easy" teacher would get a scorching lecture on the value of hard work in the educational process.

You see, Harry had been through this foolishness himself. He was born in Laredo, then moved to Irving, where he was not exactly an exemplary student in high school. But he grew up fast in Vietnam. In 1968 and '69, he served with the 5th Cavalry of the 9th Infantry Division in Vietnam. Feeling unappreciated and even scorned when he returned, he became a "biker," a leader in the "Skull Munchers," a roving band of other very scary guys—on Harleys. Among themselves, they found the respect that the country did not provide. It was a common belief, he said, that "it was a war for monetary gains for the United States and the other countries involved, to keep their economies going. So when we came back, we were treated like dirt. But we didn't lose that war," he went on. "The people who made policy lost the war. The South Vietnamese were poor fighters and interested more in graft than in winning the war. The North Vietnamese were good fighters and had good leadership. But on the battlefield we won, because we were better."

Harry graduated and I lost track of him. One day he appeared in my office. He was a graduate student in the history department at the University of Texas at Dallas. His hair was longer and he was a bit heavier. Not portly. Portly would be too soft a term for Harry.

In spirit, though, he was softer, as the pursuit of knowledge can have such an effect on a person. His face animated as he told of the wondrous things he had learned, of his duties as a teaching assistant, his plans for a career as a teacher.

He told me about his teachers, how he learned something valuable from each of them. He had been skeptical of one, though, skeptical that he could teach a course on the Vietnam War without having been there. But he did a good job, and after the class was over, he said he went up to him and told him so. "I'm sure he wasn't too interested in a compliment from a grizzled old wasted student like me, though," Harry said.

"Oh, he was interested," I assured him. Appreciative would be more like it. When Harry becomes a teacher, he will learn quickly that students like him are rare. Many like to come to college, but only a few like to learn.

· · · 🦃 · · ·

## Big Shots Get Special Treatment—Pass It On

The town leaders of Waxahachie, as in all other small towns, strive for a lack of strife. Waxahachie's natives are hard-working sons and daughters of early farmers and tradesmen who are proud of their town, their Gingerbread Trail of antebellum houses, and their ornate courthouse. They respect their civic leaders. These leaders are always referred to in the *Waxahachie Daily Light* as "prominent," which is newspaper lingo for "rich and influential."

Last week, though, a bit of hell broke loose. The *Daily Light* reported that rumors were circulating through the town that one of the banks is closing and several of its board members are under FBI investigation. "Laundering" came up a lot in the story, but you knew right off that the term didn't refer to starched shirts.

No, it was a reference to that most nefarious of terms, that most scrofulous insult, that most ignominious of accusations that could ever be leveled at a group of bankers and lawyers. These prominent men, according to the rumor, were laundering drug money!

The newspaper labored mightily and birthed a double redundancy in its Friday headline: "False rumors unfounded!" If this were a poker game, Sunday's edition could be said to have called that bit of journalistic public service and raised it one banner headline. This headline clarioned: "Bank offers $10,000 'rumor' reward," with rumor in quotation marks in case there might be one reader who doesn't understand that this is a foul and odious slander against the reputations of these upstanding townsmen, patriots all, men of fiber, all good men and true.

If this public service were not enough, the loyal publisher, inside the opinion pages, hove an indignant editorial foresquare in the faces of the evildoers who mongered these rumors. Certainly, retribution will follow, the editor wrote, as the FBI will surely punish them for wasting the Bureau's valuable time with the slanders. A small town is a place to trust your neighbor, he wrote, and rumors drive a wedge through these small-town values.

Yet just recently, this very newspaper printed an ad asking for names, addresses, and license numbers of people you might be suspicious of, people you believe to be using drugs. Just fill in the blanks and send it in to the police.

The point being... how come it is when reporters, whether with the *Waxahachie Daily Light* or the *New York Times*, want to monger a rumor about a Randall Dale Adams or a Lanell Jeter, Joyce Ann Brown, or Maurice Wells—all innocent of the crimes of which they were accused—they simply insert the word "alleged" and go home and sleep contentedly, assured that they have done all that's necessary to protect the rights of the individual? Why is it that the press waxes indignant about this only when rumors are leveled at "prominent" people?

These prominent men may, in fact, be blameless, as far as I know, and are certainly deserving of as many "alleges" as the newspaper sees fit to give them. But, in the event of a nefarious rumor assailing the name of Mr. John Q. Nonprominence, who takes out only an occasional classified ad to sell his Monte Carlo, can he expect the ink to flow in his behalf?

Most of the time, I think, he's lucky to get an "alleged."

· · · 🦃 · · ·

## The Man Who Lives on Weather

When Harold Taft first began predicting the weather for WBAP TV in Fort Worth, his main competitor was the test pattern. There was little air time in 1949 and the shows, when we got them, consisted of wrestling at North Side Coliseum, a comedian named Herb Shriner, a few westerns so old that Gabby Hayes didn't have a beard yet, and Harold, with his map and pointer.

I seldom saw him in those days, as we didn't have a television. I listened to the radio. At night, I listened to the Fort Worth Cats baseball games, announced by Bill Hightower. The Cats had such future big-league stars as Chico Carasquel, Dee Fondy, Carl Erskine, Duke Snider, and Bobby Bragan. After the games, I listened to disc jockey Zack Hert on radio station KFJZ in Fort Worth. He played all my favorite tunes, like "Cruisin' Down the River" and "My Blue Heaven." These were innocent songs for an innocent time, and I still remember their lyrics though they are anachronisms now, in an era of innocence lost.

Darwin Smith, a pal from across Buffalo Creek, had a forward-thinking dad. He bought a television that year, with a nine-inch screen. But his mom, it was said, thought it was sinful and ordered it out in the workshop behind his house. We gathered around it in the darkened shed and stared at its pale gray images. After Harold's weathercast, a man named Larry Morell came on and gave a commercial for Amanna freezers. It was all very exciting.

Harold Taft was the most memorable of all because he talked about the weather as if he believed it was more important than baseball. I had never considered such a thing before.

The Fort Worth Cats are long since defunct now; Chico Carasquel, Dee Fondy, Duke Snider, and Carl Erskine have been retired from baseball for over two decades. I haven't heard anything about Bill Hightower, Zack Hert, or Larry Morell in years. And the ten-year-old boy squinting through the darkness at the sinful flickering miracle of Darwin Smith's dad's workshop TV is a grandfather now.

Harold Taft, though, is still predicting the weather. He has never changed stations, the way he dresses, or his delivery. He has a sense of humor that emerges from time to time, but he has never appeared to like the contrived, anchor-desk happy chat in which he is obliged to participate.

Poet William Barney of Fort Worth says in his poem, "Mr. Harold Taft," that Harold has a "love affair with the elements," and that his bones "are attuned to the encroaching of seasons and circumstances." He even plays, writes Barney, "a wind instrument."

The storm that raged inside his bones has apparently run its course now, and he continues this elemental love affair on screen as he has for forty-one years. He is a "man of graphics and gauges," Barney goes on. Harold has studied the cancer as if it were a deadly weather cell system.

In this restless era of turmoil and fads, when media personalities are as disposable as last year's fashions and as generic as faces in dime-store picture frames, Harold is a model of stability.

Mrs. Smith has turned out to be as accurate in assessing the nature of television as Harold Taft has been in predicting the weather. But despite television's sins, he has made it a better medium, by giving us something a good deal more valuable than advice on whether to wash our cars or carry our umbrellas.

· · · 🐾 · · ·

# The Graduation of a Drop-Out

Lowell Andrew Dodge, our second son, graduated from college this year. This may not be such a big deal any more—a lot of people do it nowadays. But Lowell was a high school drop-out.

When he dropped out of Midlothian High School in the eleventh grade, soon after he became seventeen, we were all shocked and hurt. He had been on the honor roll at the time. I thought he might be in some kind of trouble at school, so I went up to see about it. The vice-principal, who was in charge of discipline, had never heard of Lowell. He looked up his record and was alarmed. "This doesn't make sense," he said. "Honor roll students don't quit school."

We searched for reasons. At first, Lowell was noncommittal. Eventually, he told us that he had come to hate the whole high school "scene," as he called it. He said he tried football but wasn't good enough for anything but a "blocking dummy." Though he had won several awards in junior high for his trumpet playing, he said that was no big deal in a football town. He said he was called "band fag" a lot.

He said he tried to find one of the cliques he could fit into. The "jocks" club was out. Band, too. What was left were the "goat-ropers," the "dopers," and the "preppies." He said he chose the "preppies" and wore all the over-priced designer clothes and went to the wild parties before finally coming to view it all as pointless.

Another factor: his steady girlfriend at the time had already graduated.

So he just stopped going. I would drop him off on my way to work, and he would come back home. Once, I didn't go in to work until later but instead came back home. Lowell was already there. I forced him back into the car and returned him to school. He beat me back home again.

The school is little different from the public school I attended in Cleburne or from the one where I taught in Mansfield. As a college teacher, I labored for twenty-six years to encourage young high school graduates to think for themselves—a new and frightening experience for them. It was the hardest part of my job. Lowell, a free-thinker, would not have flourished in any other public school I know of. They stress conformity, obedience, and punctuality. They control hairstyles, fashions, and ideas with equal zeal. Questioning of standard opinions and mores is always problematical in institutions emphasizing socialization over learning. His older brother and sister, who have more conventional social skills, graduated from this school with good records. Thousands of others have too. The school has a good standing throughout the state.

We were all saddened by his quitting, but we never doubted that he would succeed. I took comfort knowing that the lack of a high school diploma did not deter Thomas Edison, Mark Twain, or Henry Ford. Even a governor of New York and a presidential nominee had no diploma. His mother was not consoled by this information.

Lowell's degree at Mountain View College is in electronics technology, his proficiency for which has already brought him work. His major professor, Dr. Stan Fulton, told me he was among their top ten graduates of the past ten years. He recommended him as a co-op student-employee at National Semiconductor in Arlington, where he now works as a senior technician. Not long ago, they gave him an outstanding employee award.

Lowell made good despite his weakness in the area of "fitting in" and despite the public school system's reluctance to accommodate unconventionality. "I like to learn," he said, "but I don't like to go to high school."

He made it anyway. But too many like him don't. The problems with public education only mirror a society that seems to define the pursuit of happiness as chasing the dollar, hurrying to the mall, and keeping up with the ball scores. Real learning requires constant questioning, experimentation, and testing—of both student and teacher. Education should hurt. Brain building is like body building: no pain, no gain.

An undue emphasis on conformity and conventional wisdom may be harmless for some students, but what do you do with those like Lowell, who want to learn but don't want to be controlled?

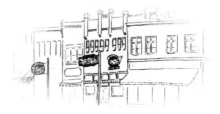

# 1991

*We Texans must endeavor to stop putting an "r" in "warsh" and put it at the end of Cuba, where newcomers from Boston seem to think it belongs.*

## Uncle Dock

World War I was not bloodless and impersonal as modern wars are. Many young soldiers died. As a boy, I learned about this war's horror from my grandmother, whose twin brother, Andrew Jackson James, was killed in France, just weeks before the armistice. He was twenty-two, a mannerly farm boy, when he was called. He knew nothing of fighting; he wanted to be a Baptist minister.

Today he would qualify as a conscientious objector. But he went, and he became a medical corpsman. In the photographs he sent home, he stands proud and straight in his uniform. Wearing his customary round, wire-rimmed glasses, he looks eerily like Woodrow Wilson, the president my family blamed for that war.

It was a particularly brutal time for my grandmother. When Uncle Dock was drafted she had a three-year-old boy, also a baby boy with measles, and was eight months pregnant with my mother. The baby died in March of 1918, when my mother was one month old. My grandfather was near death with typhoid fever. They lived on a squalid sandy-land farm near Egan, in Johnson County, with no running water. Neighbors helped care for my grandfather and helped get in the crops.

During the Gulf War, I re-read the thirty-five fragile, brown and chipped letters Uncle Dock wrote to his family on YMCA stationary. They chronicle his final seven months of life.

He tried to raise my grandmother's spirits. My grandfather's fever would break, he told her, and God would protect them all. The baby was in heaven and out of pain. Someday, when the war is over, he would be home, and he would pay them out of debt with the money he saved. He asked, usually, about his colt and asked once if someone would send him a picture of it. "Is it big enough to ride?" he asked.

He described the wonders he saw in faraway places like Atlanta, San Antonio, New Jersey, and New York. From San Antonio, he wrote that he had seen the Alamo and the "big parks up here with nothing in them but animals." He had never heard of a zoo. On his trip north, he said he "crossed a river about 4 miles wide, I guess," and that he had seen "one steamboat." For his father, he described the crops he saw from the window of his troop train.

By September of 1918, he was in France. From "somewhere in the mountains," he wrote that he had taken "a case of the blues" but, as always, was "trusting in God's protection." He would be home in time to eat "Xmas dinner," he wrote, and they could "all be happy together and sit around and talk it over."

His letters are never political or patriotic. He did not pretend to know what the war meant but never questioned it. Letters from a friend, Carson Behringer, from near Whitney, praise his courage "in this great fight for freedom" and urge him to help eradicate the "evil Kaisar over there." Behringer had been paralyzed in a diving accident, and Uncle Dock had stayed by him during his critical period of pneumonia. Letters from Ethyl Biffel, a friend from Sunday school, apprise Uncle Dock of church doings in Meridian.

In his final letter home, he wrote, "I am praying for you mother, and for all the rest. I dream of being at home very often." Closing, he added, "I will meet you in heaven."

In late October of 1918, a telegram addressed to Mrs. Sarah James advised her that "Andrew Jackson James was killed in France on or near September 26, 1918, by falling bombshells."

A Bureau of War Risk insurance policy for $10,000, signed by the Secretary of the Treasury, arrived on March 1, 1919. It named her and his twin sister, my grandmother, as co-beneficiaries and was to be paid in monthly installments of $57.

A faded Fort Worth *Star-Telegram* story describes him as "the first Johnson County soldier killed in the Great War."

My great-grandmother James was embittered, I was told, and flung the medals at the officers who brought them and cursed the insurance money. She slipped into senility soon after that and died a few years later.

As Uncle Dock had predicted, my grandfather's fever broke, my grandmother, in time, came to accept the baby's death, and his as well. Uncle Dock's insurance money paid them out of debt and brought them through the Depression.

He has many relatives still living in Johnson and Hill Counties. My mother works at the First Baptist Church, where he might have preached one day if he had lived. My grandparents died in the 1980s and are buried at Caddo Cemetery near Godley, alongside my grandfather's parents, two of his brothers, and the baby Howard. My grandfather bought that lot in 1918 for five dollars.

Just a few steps away, on the hill between his mother and father, sleeps Andrew James, the "first Johnson County soldier killed in the Great War."

· · · ❦ · · ·

# Look Upward, Angel

I went to bed after reading a news item about the poor performance by Texas schoolchildren on math and reading tests. I dreamed that I visited the big school ground in the sky. I was welcomed at this celestial campus by a venerable scholar in a mortarboard. "Where have you been?" he said, embracing me with the most magnificent pair of wings I had ever seen. "The children have been waiting for you."

All around the campus pupils drifted about happily on clouds, discussing topics such as natural law and government by popular consent. Conspicuously missing were security guards walking patrol with their drug dogs. Also, there were no metal detectors or administrators monitoring student fashions. "How can you have school without these?" I said.

"Oh, we don't need them here," he said. "We are interested only in ideas and spiritual self-discovery. We de-emphasize the needs of the body since we don't have them. Makes it easier for the students to concentrate." He smiled. "But we do have recreation." To demonstrate, he showed me fluffy playing fields where boys and girls engaged in friendly games of wing-walking, to see who could stay aloft longest without flapping their wings. Also message bearing, a friendly competition to see who was the fastest at delivering glad tidings. And their favorite game of all, halo-toss.

"But how do you get away with ignoring all the machismo sports? What about football?"

"Oh, we don't have football because it wouldn't be very interesting. The brightest of the boys, the ones with the longest wings, would simply fly over everybody and make all the scores. And besides," he added, grinning impishly, "most of the coaches go to the, uh, other place."

I couldn't believe it. No football? How can the little boys please their dads and get recognition up here? What about cheerleaders?

"We learned from our previous lives," he said, "that such activities emphasize differences between the boys and the girls at a critical time in their development and teach the boys that physical strength is the way to get respect and teaches the girls that cheering is the way to please the boys. Later on, as you know, some men use their physical strength against women because they think they don't cheer for them enough."

"Instead," he went on, "since the body falls away, we emphasize the importance of our *eternal* attributes." He led me to a large downy cloud in the center of the campus. Inside, it was resplendent with all the colors of the rainbow. "It is a cosmic studio," he told me. "Here, we make every child a star, every day, forever. Their every achievement is heralded with rejoicing and exultation—a kind of celestial high-five. Each child is spotlighted in the 'Brain' section of the *Hallelujah Times Eternal News*, and they all hope to get into the I.Q. Hall of Fame."

He directed my attention to popular entertainment the children watched in their leisure time. They were crowded around a two-thousand-foot-wide TV screen, watching "The Super I.Q. Bowl," showing teams of cherubic savants filling the rarified air with erudition. On another cloud floating by, a group listened to "The Wide World of Bach."

I must have looked dumbfounded. "Back on earth," he told me, "people *say* they want a good education for their children but they really want them to be sports stars. They even send these athletes to college free on programs call *scholar*ships instead of calling them 'athletic grants'—which would be somewhat more accurate."

"Will education back in America ever improve?"

My celestial guide smiled at me to hide a perceptible exasperation. "I'm sorry to have to tell you this," he said, "but you don't really want it to improve. At least, not enough to demonstrate it to the children. You still have two sections in your newspapers devoted only to sports. Children want to get recognition, so athletics is what they do to get it. With children," he went on, "you always get the behavior that you reward. You have great football players because this is what you emphasize."

"But, but—can't you have both?"

"You will always get the behavior that you reward," he said.

"But, but—"

Suddenly, he receded—and I woke up chanting: "You always get the behavior that you reward." It's so simple! Why hadn't I thought of it before?

A better question: Why are the simplest solutions hardest to see?

· · · 🍎 · · ·

## Art and Patriotism

During the final week of the Gulf War, I was the speaker at the Creative Arts Fair at Southwest Texas State Jr. College at Uvalde. Each year the college sponsors this event to encourage artists from kindergarten to the nursing home.

Hundreds of brightly colored paintings covered the auditorium walls. The art was beautiful and inspiring. A large table held the trophies to be awarded to the participants. Everyone would win something, it seemed.

There would be about five hundred people there, and it would be appropriate to say something to encourage them to continue with their art, the dean said. By the way, it is a very "conserva-tive" audience, he added.

David England is a rarity among deans. He knows the impor-tance of the creative arts, as he is a writer himself. He directed me to a computer in a quiet place to write my speech. I looked at the blank screen for a while without writing a word. All I could think about was how inspiring all these paintings were. But none of this inspiration seemed to find its way onto the screen.

Finally, I managed to write two words: "The End." Then, I got up and went into the auditorium to watch the people come in. Proud parents with their small children. Young girls with the latest MTV look. Teenaged boys in their buckaroo duds and pooched-out snuff lips. Anglo and Hispanic, all excited and proud.

When Dean England introduced me, I strode to the podium with all the assurance of a jaywalker. I looked around the room. Most of the children were staring at the trophy table, imagining no doubt, how great they were going to look in their rooms. Most of their parents seemed to eye me warily. I knew they would not be impressed by some learned prolegomenon on the nature of the artistic experience, even if I would be able to inflict one on them.

So instead, I just told them how beautiful all the paintings lin-ing the walls were and how moved I was by the talent of the artists. I told them how uplifting it was to see such a turnout in support of an activity so constructive and so life-affirming as art when many of our government leaders were doing their best to stifle it, and at a time when there was so much destruction and devastation in another part of the world.

I don't think they appreciated that analogy as much as I wanted them to. I felt a tension building and making its way around the room before finally settling in my throat. I finished by encouraging them to continue with their art, as there could never be too many *con*structive activities in this very *de*structive world.

They applauded politely. They knew the value of respect, even though they hadn't liked the overtones of my remarks. These are not people ever to be inhospitable to guests.

Was I disrespectful to them for raising this political analogy when they clearly had come only to have a good time and pick up their trophies without having to think about such serious subjects? On the return home, I was still pondering this question when a quotation popped into my head: "No one has the right to interfere with the simple beliefs of the people." When I considered the implications of this quotation I was heartened that I had done right.

The man who wrote this, Adolph Hitler, hated all thought —and all art—not approved by the state. Sometimes, learning cannot occur without interfering with the "simple beliefs of the people."

· · · ❦ · · ·

# Handicapped Parking Space Addicts

A recent newspaper column on the subject of handicapped parking elicited a few bitter chuckles from members of the Dodge family. We've learned over the years to view this utter fascination some able-bodied people have with handicapped parking spaces with the equanimity reserved for other human failings.

When Lindon first inched his way back into the real world after his paralyzing accident in 1982, it didn't take long for us to learn that he would have to compete with the able-bodied for the handicapped spaces. They always had a ready excuse: "I was just running in for a minute," or they answered contemptuously, "I'm handicapped. Why don't you mind your own business!" A man was quoted in the column as saying that he was "tired of hiking in from the north forty when there were too many handicapped spaces going unused."

Other handicapped aspirants complained that they were afflicted with various ailments that necessitated the coveted spaces. One young woman said she had undergone a lot of physical therapy in order to walk without a limp but was nevertheless entitled to the space. The question coming to mind is why, if she wants to hide her handicap, is she so eager to park in the handicap zone? Others quoted in the piece said more or less the same things, that their handicaps made them eligible even though they may not be apparent.

This is certainly true in some cases. But too many physicians give permits when they shouldn't. Sometimes people get them for a temporary ailment and keep them forever. Police are reluctant to cite these offenses because they don't want to get into the game of deciding who's really handicapped and who's not.

Lindon seldom uses the handicapped spaces. He tries to ignore them because they are too often occupied by someone with a handicap no more disabling than an inflamed hangnail, and he doesn't want to see this. Or he's afraid he might take a space that someone needs more than he needs it. He tries instead to locate a space somewhere that he thinks it is less likely that he will be pinned inside his car. He doesn't need a space up close; he needs only for it to be wide enough for him to get his wheelchair out without damaging someone's car. Pushing a hundred yards doesn't bother him; he likes to do everything he is able to do.

What is this obsession these healthy people have with handicapped spaces? Are they really this lazy? Is it simply hypochondriacs longing for attention? Is it people pretending they are celebrities with their own reserved parking spaces? Or are they just selfish, spoiled children, taking the spaces because they can get away with it?

Whatever the reason, it's embedded in their psyches and should be studied by psychologists.

Lindon believes that the only way to keep unauthorized people out of these spaces is to place the spaces farther back in the parking lots. As long as the spaces are wide enough, the handicapped will be satisfied. And they will no longer have to compete for the spaces with the handicapped parking space addicts. The addicts won't go near them if they're "back in the north forty."

They hate walking.

· · · ❦ · · ·

## Will There Be Life After Bingo

My Aunt Bernice says the lottery has ruined her life.

She blames northerners for it, along with just about everything else that goes wrong, though I've tried to tell her about all the good things our friends from that other country have given us. Before they came to Texas, we didn't have shopping on Sunday, cable TV, horseracing, or bankruptcy privileges. We thought a BMW was some kind of odd bathroom habit.

We're also obliged to them for the easy way they insinuated themselves into positions of responsibility in our corporations, media, schools, politics, and massage parlors.

This is fine with most Texans because we'd rather be sitting on the screened-in front porch jawing with each other about the kinfolks than rummaging through any old briefcase looking for flow charts and policy manuals.

Shoot, I told her, now we can just put in our eight hours and get back to the house in time for *Hee-Haw*.

Aunt Bernice nodded in agreement but said that what was almost as bad for her as this lottery was their danged palaver. She was referring to the time she told her son-in-law, who is from Michigan, that if you bought a carton of Phillip Morris down at the Buy on the Fly, they will give you a free "ladder." Son-in-law, who is always on the lookout for a bargain, leaped into his BMW and lit out for the Buy on the Fly to get his free "ladder."

When he came back he said, "I thought you said that if I bought a carton of Phillip Morris down at the Buy on the Fly that they'd give me a free ladder!"

Aunt Bernice looked at him with astonishment, then flicked her Bic in his face and said, "That's exactly what I said—a *cigarette ladder!*"

But unlike Aunt Bernice, I'm greatly obliged to them for the new lingo. For example, I used to think the evening meal was supper. Now I know it's dinner, which I had been mistakenly eating at noon for all those years.

I used to call the top of my house a roof. Now I know it's a ruff, though I'm somewhat confused about what to call that part of the golf course that doctors and lawyers hit their golf balls into.

I now say I'm able to do something, rather than "I might could." And I try to refrain from calling up other members of the *Linguisticus Texanicus* species and saying, "What are y'all doing?" But this is an old tradition, dating back to the Pleistocene epoch, and one very hard to break.

Also, when something belongs to us, we say it's "ires," instead of ours. The latter is what we count when we're watching the clock at work. Like Ross Perot, I still say "mihyuns" instead of "millllions," stretching out the "l's" as Carl Sagan does. Though Carl pronounces it correctly, old Ross has more of them.

I'm trying to stop "warshing" my pickup. Newcomers from Massachusetts are amused by this. We Texans must endeavor to leave the "r" out of "warsh" and put it at the end of "Cuba" where Bostonians seem to think it belongs.

Speaking of improvement, I'm doing my part for the rehabilitation of "window." The other day I heard a small, ungrammatical kid of the *Texanicus* persuasion say to his pal, "Let's chunk a rock through Old Man Dodge's winda light." Right there's when I set him straight.

"No, young man," I pointed out, "you mean you wish to cast a stone through Old Man Dodge's window pane!"

Aunt Bernice may be indifferent to these commercial and linguistic changes, but she's adamant about the lottery. "Oh lord," she said, when she heard about the great numbers playing it and the vast amounts in the jackpots. "The next thing you know, they'll take over bingo!"

· · · 🍎 · · ·

## Elvis and My Little Darlin's

In Cleburne during the 1950s, we always looked forward to October. This meant the World Series, the Texas-Oklahoma football game, and the State Fair in Dallas. We just called it The Fair, or sometimes, the Dallas Fair.

Actually, that's pretty much what it has been since its inception over a hundred years ago. With revenues of over $100 million for Dallas each year, the State Fair is second only to Christmas as a religious event.

The Fair of 1956 would prove to be especially religious for the teenaged girls of Cleburne. Elvis was coming. To the rest of the world, he wasn't The King yet, but he was to our girls.

A week before, a relatively obscure pitcher named Don Larson had pitched a perfect game for the Yankees against the Dodgers in the World Series. I endeavored to discuss this historic event with my girlfriends, but, inexplicably to me at the time, they preferred to talk about their elaborate plans to see Elvis.

The boys loved him too, but we would never admit this to the girls. "He's not so hot," my argument went. "He's certainly no Sinatra. Why, when Sinatra opened at the Paramount Theatre in New York in 1941, thousands of girls got heart attacks—and died! It's not good to get so worked up liked that," I warned them. "I'm not going. I'm going to see Victor Borge instead. You should, too. He's ten times better than some old truck driver with oily hair."

But of course my psychology failed, and on that momentous night, hundreds of teenaged girls in hoop-skirts fetched their fathers' binoculars and squeezed into cars driven by desperate mothers and headed east on Highway 67, bound for pelvis-pumping, hip-gyrating, lip-curling, ducktailed glory at the Cotton Bowl. This convoy of ecstasy formed at the courthouse and reached all the way to back on West Henderson Street to the football stadium.

Where were we, the boys of Cleburne High? We were at Carl Chafin's cafe, in the back booths, love-bereft and undone by Elvis, smothering our sorrow in cheeseburgers. "We shoulda went," somebody finally said. "They're going without us. Now what are we gonna do?"

Through the window we watched the last of the Elvis convoy carrying our little darlin's cross Main Street and disappear, maybe forever, into the hazy gloom of that small-town Elvis

Presley afternoon. Maybe they would be changed when they came back. Could a young girl ever be the same after seeing those lips, those hips in motion? What about our less-animated hips, our renditions of "Blueberry Hill," our flat-top haircuts they had once thought so cool and had so thrilled them before? Someone finally expressed the unthinkable: "What kind of mothers are they gonna make now?"

These were questions we had to confront over more cheeseburgers and milkshakes until the girls came back.

Thankfully, they did come back—and they weren't ruined forever. "They had him behind a high fence," they said. "Nobody could get close enough to touch him."

Thank god for fences! I said to myself.

The Fair came and went that year, and things returned to normal in my hometown. The girls went back to the excitement of school dances and movies down at the Esquire Theatre and smooching with us out at Moonspot. A few years later, I found the one I wanted and we got married.

Thanks Elvis, for not ruining my little darlin'.

· · · 🐞 · · ·

# You Can't Go Home Again But You Can Bike to Grandview

We all remember where we were when Kennedy was shot or when Neil Armstrong stepped onto the moon, but you have to be a baseball fan to know where you were on October 3, 1951. This was the day Bobby Thompson hit the home run that became known as the other "shot heard 'round the world."

It was a State Fair day for the Cleburne schools, but I wasn't going. For me it would be a baseball day. I had my radio tuned to KLIF where the "Old Scotsman," Gordon McLendon, would be calling the play by play for the game at the Polo Grounds in New York between the Brooklyn Dodgers and the New York Giants. The Giants won 38 of their last 46 games and tied the Dodgers for the National League title on the final day of the season. Each had won a game in the three-game play-off. The Dodgers lineup that day was loaded with stars—Reese, Hodges, Campanella, Cox, Snider, and Robinson. Pitching against Giants ace Sal Maglie was the indomitable Don Newcombe. In the Giants outfield was a young player with promise named Willie Mays.

The hero of this game, however, would be a lesser light among all these luminaries. Bobby Thompson would be the name that would go down in baseball history. And I was all set to hear it.

But I had a best friend, William Parnell, who wasn't a baseball fan. He talked me into going for a bike ride. We would be back before the game started, he said. It was a bright, crisp day as we rode along the Grandview highway. Our fun was so absorbing that we lost track of time and mileage and, I couldn't believe my eyes, Grandview lay ahead. We had ridden thirteen miles, and I had missed the game!

I rushed into Huffman's Drug Store downtown. The radio was on, and a few customers were listening to the game. It was the ninth inning!

The Dodgers were winning four to two. Newcomb had just been replaced on the mound by Ralph Branca. Two Giants runners were on base. Thompson comes up. You can hardly hear the Old Scotsman over the crowd. "They're going to be talking about this game for years to come," he says. Thomson takes a pitch, then hits the next one into the left field seats. The Old Scotsman's voice is all but obscured by the roar. In the background you can hear him say, "The Giants win the pennant! The Giants win the pennant! Well, I'll be a suck-egg mule!"

Thirty years later to the day, William and I commemorated that occasion by riding our bikes from Cleburne to Grandview. His parents and his ninety-two-year-old grandmother saw us off from St. Paul's Methodist Church on East Henderson Street. The house I lived in on English Street behind the church is still standing, and Pete Kendell, the sports editor for the *Cleburne Times Review*, came and took our picture in front of it for the newspaper.

Grannie squeezed William's tires, checking his "caissons" for air pressure, and then we set out—in search of our past on Highway 4 to Grandview.

It was a warm day with a pleasant breeze, bringing the scent of broomweed from the fields along the way. William, always a student of history and Indian life, pointed out the fields where he had searched for arrowheads back then. There were new houses along the way and a lot more cars on the highway. We tried to locate the house with the well in the front yard where we had stopped and gotten a drink, but there were too many houses now. On the first ride, Bobby Rogers, a high school boy, had passed us in his 1936 Ford and waved. We saw him as he came back toward home and we weren't halfway to Grandview yet. I remember thinking how great is must be to be grown up and have a nice car. He's a banker now and has an even better car. I wish he had passed us on our second ride.

But he didn't—and Huffman's Drug Store no longer existed either. So we went across the street to the Main Street Café to eat lunch and listen to the final inning of the game on a tape given to me by the Old Scotsman himself.

On the ride back, it occurred to me that we hadn't really changed at all. I had lost hair and his had turned white. We had gained some weight and our joints ached a bit more—but beneath all that we were the same kids as before. I'm still writing about sports, and William still searches for arrowheads—on digs with the an archeology club.

Maybe we didn't recapture our past that day, but the memory of a baseball game brought us back together. What we did recapture was our friendship that we had misplaced somewhere among the careers and wives and children and grandchildren and mortgages and aspirations and tragedies that somehow seem to take precedence over other things, as O. Henry says, during the seventy years or so that immediately precede our funerals.

$$\cdots \; \text{🐞} \; \cdots$$

# Whole Wheat Nonzense

Garland writer Jim Wheat is engaging in the higher forms of literary mayhem again, and it may be too late to stop him.

One of his recent books, *Shouting in a Vacuum*, made it all the way to England where Penguin Books appropriated some of his contraband syllogisms, belated premonitions, and advance recollections from that book for a volume of verse for teenagers.

The October issue of *National Lampoon* contains one of Wheat's mock album release promos, a genre for which he is infamous among his fans. The "album," entitled "Let's Grow Hair," carries a likeness of "Dean Don Durbin" in a black cowboy hat and looking like a womperjawed, goofy Hopalong Cassidy. It features such Durbin "hits" as "Lockjaw Polka," "He's Gone to Get Jesus," and "The Devil Ate His Taters."

In numerous self-published chapbooks from his Nonzense Press, Wheat parodies not only music and movie reviews but also the news, crossword puzzles, advice columns, opinion polls, maps, grocery ads, critics, people who take themselves too seriously, and everybody else. These titles include *Gumbo, Uh-Oh, I Ain't Through Laughing, Bringing Home the Moon, Spook, I Won't Tell a Soul,* and *Faster Than Gone.*

A selection of Wheat's inscrutable sophistries includes:

- "Show me a man and a woman and I'll show you her husband."
- "An open door closes both ways."
- "Give a fool another chance—he gave you one."
- "I'm sorry, I thought you were famous."
- "He was taller in the rear, but he leaned up in front."
- "Stand back, my pants are falling down."
- "It takes an honest man to steal his own watch."
- "If you have any questions you know more than me."

This latter Wheaticism raises a good point about his writings. Maybe too much education is a deterrent to deciphering them. A friend of mine, Dr. Paul Benson, who is a fan of Wheat's, frets over his inability to uncover the "exigencies" of Wheat's books. He is a professor and has a doctor's degree. He earns his living by explaining things, many of them complicated and arcane. Mysteries ought to have solutions, he believes, conundrums should be explainable, and books ought to make sense. Yet, on a shelf in his office sits a copy of James Joyce's *Finnegans Wake.* In a newspaper on his desk, there is a photo of Nancy Reagan sitting on Mr. T's lap. A news magazine in his office carries a story stating that the NAACP will oppose the nomination of a black judge to the Supreme Court.

Children, though, seem automatically to understand the wisdom of nonsense. When I spoke to my daughter's fourth-graders, I read them a selection of Wheaticisms. They enjoyed them with great velocity—so great that the principal came to quell the outbreak of fun. At the end of the period, the children were still laughing. "Stand back," they were saying, "my pants are falling down!"

Dr. Benson knows that the world is incomprehensible much of the time, of course, but points out that some of the time it seems almost rational. "Jimmy never comes out of Oz, though," he adds.

Or out of his house, for that matter. He's publicity-shy and, at forty-three, still lives with his parents. Why hasn't he ever left home? "No dough!" he says.

"I was shy in high school," he says, "but I got witty in junior college, which I attended for three weeks."

When I am sometimes bewildered by people's behavior or have used all my skills to analyze a problem and the "exigencies" of it still elude me, then I try to apply this bit of wisdom from *Spout:*

"Oh, dear, I'm afraid I've lost my glasses."

"Where have you looked for them?"

"I've looked everywhere I can think of."

"Maybe they're lost in a place you can't find."

"Nope. I looked there too."

"Then maybe *you're* lost."

If I still don't get it, then I try to remember, as Wheat says, that "nothing makes sense until you least expect it."

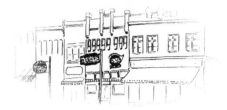

# 1992

*You might be surprised by the improvement $27,000
stuffed into the lapel pocket can make on the
appearance of a polyester suit.*

## The Warren Beatty of Dogs

Four has been in that big dog run in the sky for over a year now. He lost a battle with old age and a very big dog. But I still miss him as I would any other close friend.

R. P. Dexter, friend of mine and friend of all dogs, came over and helped me bury him in my hedgerow. The veterinarian had finished what the very big dog wasn't able to accomplish. Four was wrapped tightly in gauze, and Dex said he looked like a small mummy.

The children said he was part pig and part 'possum, but I say he was a dog. He barked and had the head of a dog, and I'm pretty sure he was a dog. But he *was* shaped like a pig, and he had the lust of a politician or Warren Beatty. This latter attribute kept him away from home a lot. When he wasn't sparking some friendly female he was in the dog hospital recovering from the consequences of love.

Being born as an afterthought gave him his name. His three siblings arrived early one evening. But the next morning we checked, and there he was. We named them One, Two, Three, and Four. Lowell Dodge, only eight at the time, had a riddle:

"How come Midget had four puppies; we gave three away and still got Four?"

Four turned out to be a mama's boy, and bigger dogs beat him up a lot. But it was his girlfriends' owners that gave him the most pain. They seemed dedicated to ridding the Midlothian community of the long, low dog with the super libido. Once he came home with a broken jaw, apparently administered by the owner of some unspayed canine coquette whose honor Four had allegedly violated. He looked like he had been hit by a truck.

In fact, a truck did hit him once, breaking his shoulder and ribcage and puncturing a lung. He went around in a full body cast with one front leg pointing out forward. The air leaked out of his lung and collected under his skin. If he hadn't been weighted down with plaster he would have gone airborne. He tried to go out sparking in this condition but fell over a lot. Aside from the broken jaw, shoulder, ribcage, and punctured lung, he also had a hernia from a collision with the top of a backyard fence during a hasty getaway, and there was no hair on his back from too many tight squeezes under fences. He had scars all over his little pig body from the whippings of the angry owners of these little hormonal coquettes, and not a few gunshot wounds.

One tranquil winter eve we were in the den, I in my nightcap and slippers, contemplating the happiness of suburban life, and old Four, in mid-life and therefore somewhat less libidinous, lazing contentedly by the fireplace. Suddenly, the tranquillity was rent asunder and every which way by Four's desperate and unceasing howling. Nothing could quiet him. So there was little choice but to gather him up and rush him to the veterinarian, who I had alerted and was waiting for us at the clinic.

X-rays showed that a small bullet resulting from some long-forgotten tryst had lodged in his hind leg and resided there harmlessly for years. The heat from the fireplace, theorized the vet, had caused the pellet to travel, coming to rest painfully against the nearest nerve. The consequence of a forbidden pleasure from long ago had finally reached its mark. I suffered too. Its extraction cost me a hundred bucks.

After that, Four's trysting slowed down. But he could still muster enough dog testosterone to get himself into trouble. A memorable such occasion landed him in dog jail. He had been gone a week; then his picture showed up in a Sunday edition of the *Waxahachie Daily Light*. "Come and get me," the caption said. "I wanna go home."

The dog jail was closed on Sunday, but I drove over anyway. I yelled out his name and about a dozen little dog-faced guys popped up from behind a fenced wall. The final one, on the end, last in the pecking order, was Four. The next morning I went over first thing and bailed him out—twenty-eight bucks. Several of his cellmates beat him up one last time, but he didn't care—he was getting sprung.

His last dalliance may have been his most dramatic. I remember the phone message: "Mr. Dodge, I have a long, low dog in my backyard and I believe he belongs to you. He came in my yard and [did something unprintable to] two of my Pomeranians. I would appreciate it if you would come down to the vet clinic and pay for the pregnancy interventions." When I did this, he went on, I could have my dog back.

Well, I went down and paid for Four's alleged misconduct. Then, receipt in hand, I stopped by to get him.

"He's escaped," the guy said, pointing to a knawed-out hole in the bottom of his cedar fence.

When I got home, Four was sitting in the driveway, smoking a cigarette.

Not really, but he did seem to be embarrassed, as if trying to say that he never touched those girls.

I realize that because of the way Four was allowed to live his life, I will receive warranted lectures from people with a lot more knowledge than I have about good pet care and pet citizenship. I know now that Four should have been separated from his little dog testicles so that he would not have caused havoc among my neighbors and issued into the world any more replicas of himself. I realize that about the only people in the county who weren't happy to hear of Four's leavetaking were the veterinarians. Actually, he had multipage, single-spaced medical charts in three counties—Ellis, Johnson, and Dallas.

Four was a rounder, this is true. But he paid for it and seldom complained. He was also funny and had a good personality. He was a good friend and traveling companion. Everybody in our family has a good Four story. One was that when Four went to a dog motel he went incognito and signed his name, "Three Plus One." Sometimes, just "Two Plus Two." When he was feeling down, maybe "Five Minus One."

I hope that where Four is now there are lots of frisky females and no neighbors wielding guns and brickbats. I hope he has lots of old tires and posts and a bladder that never runs dry.

· · · ❦ · · ·

# Shut Up and Watch Television

When I started teaching in 1965, my students at Mansfield High School read, with relative ease, *Crime and Punishment*, *Moby Dick*, *Les Miserables*, and *Silas Marner*. By 1970, though I was teaching college students at Mountain View College in Dallas, I had dropped these classics from my lesson plans. Most students found them too difficult for the ever-decreasing time they had in their lives for reading.

The students of today believe in the benefits of reading and wish they liked to read. They have been bombarded all their lives with the importance of reading. They probably have guilt because they don't read as much as they feel they should. Why they don't read very much is a complex question.

For them, television and movies have replaced books as entertainment. They feel these are more entertaining than reading and require less time. Almost everybody under the age of fifty grew up with a television in the household. Movies have been around for the entire twentieth century. For most people, these are their primary modes of entertainment. Movies can tell a story as well as a book can, just in a different way. As films, *The Grapes of Wrath* and *To Kill a Mockingbird* are works of storytelling art on the level with the novels. *The Godfather* and *A Passage to India* are even better as films than they are as books. Children should not be scolded for preferring these movies. Instead, they need a better reason for reading than that it is good for them. They need to be taught the value of *words*.

They have little understanding of the nature of language or that words have histories and undergo evolution. As I call roll the first time each semester, I find that most students don't even know that their surnames have histories and meanings. They don't know that the names of their hometowns have histories and meanings. They've never thought about it. Shouldn't they be learning this, beginning in the first grade?

In reading, words are the building blocks of images. Thinking is vital to making this connection. Imagination and fantasy are also necessary. Television and movies provide images ready-made. I recently watched an MTV cartoon with a young viewer named Amy while a muscular woman in an iron bikini killed hundreds of goons with an automatic weapon. "What does this mean?" I asked.

"Don't think about it," she told me. "Just watch it."

Students need also to be told that it is all right to read whatever they like. I realize that many parents and educators will disagree, as no one wants children to read the writings of the Marquis de Sade and the like. But most students won't do this. If by chance a child should read such books excessively, it would be a symptom of some abberation of the brain that was already present. Youthful curiosity about death, sex, witches, vampires, and other taboo subjects is normal and will pass—again, provided that the child's psyche is healthy. You can't improve a disturbed child's mental condition by censoring books. So it is a mistake, I believe, for parents and teachers to dictate what students should read. All of us want to read books that reflect the inner workings of our brains.

When parents and teachers dictate what a student reads, they are saying, "I identify with this book, and you should too." It doesn't work this way. Allowing others to read books that reflect them encourages them to read. As they grow, their interests will change and so will the books they read. As a boy, I read thousands of comic books, all of Thomas C. Hinkle's dog and horse books, J. Frank Dobie's books about lost mines and cattle trails, biographies of Jim Bridger, Kit Carson, and the like. (Also, as many of the "salacious" novels of Mickey Spillane that I could get my hands on.) But I was generally indifferent to my classroom reading assignments, such as *Paradise Lost*. As I grew older and my experiences and curiosities broadened, I came to appreciate these classics more. Now, I read them almost exclusively. In college, though, I heard a professor say that you shouldn't even attempt to read *Paradise Lost* until you're at least sixty years old.

I swore a solemn oath that I would not and, so far, I have been able to keep this covenant.

What this professor meant was, that most people cannot appreciate this book at a young age. A book, then, is a mirror, and if you don't see a pleasing image of yourself reflected in it, then just keep reading until you do.

· · · ❦ · · ·

## When Superman Dies

When teachers die, it is hardly ever page-one news. They don't go down in a blaze of gunfire while defending against the forces of evil, as police officers do, or soldiers. But when they die, their comrades turn out to pay tribute because they know they, too, have fought the forces of evil. There is no evil worse than ignorance. When they come in tribute, they are as low-key and unsentimental as they are in the classrooms. And ironically, it is not uncommon for teachers, who have spent their professional lives teaching about the need for ritual, myth, and symbol, to dispense with funerals altogether.

Steve Turner stated in his will that there should be no public display of his leavetaking, no memorial service, only that his ashes be scattered over the Pacific. His family would honor this request for the disposition of his ashes, but they had to have a memorial. They needed it, and rightly so.

The chapel at Arlington was filled. Many were professors from the University of Texas at Arlington, where Steve had taught from 1960 to 1982. Old friend and colleague George Fortenberry spoke and read from *A Measure of Dust*, Steve's novel that came out in 1970. With the passages he selected, he helped us reflect on the depth and breadth of Steve's heart and mind and brought laughs by his recollections of their times together.

Afterward, I tried to recall what it was that made Steve such a good writing teacher. He wasn't a dramatic lecturer; he had a soft southern accent and a conversational delivery. He hardly marked our assignments. There was nothing about his technique that administrators would call innovative. In fact, he pointedly distanced himself from whatever was currently fashionable among educational experts. And he frequently violated their "retention" policy by being gruff with lazy students. He didn't believe that you were helping them or the college by coddling them. Boys in his classes stayed awake and kept their heels off the desks or they were soon cooling them outside. Steve, in one of his many other jobs, had been a bouncer.

Of course, I liked him because he encouraged me to write. He sometimes read excerpts from my stories in class. "Pretty good stuff here," he would say. Coming from Steve, this equaled any other teacher's offer to go on your note and pay your tuition at Harvard. Once, I hadn't particularly liked his theme topics so I wrote a review of *A Measure of Dust*. He groused at first about this but ended up giving me credit for it. He wouldn't give me a grade, though. He didn't want vanity to be involved.

For me, he was a memorable teacher because he was a model of everything I wanted to be. I wanted to be a writer. Not only did I want to have a novel published by Simon and Schuster, but I wanted to be tall and broad-shouldered and athletic and good-looking like him and drink my whiskey neat. I wished I had been at Pearl Harbor, been a boxer, a bartender, bouncer, actor, and had all the women wrapped around my little finger. And of course, I wanted to be modest about all this, as he was.

I wanted to have my prize-winning play presented at the William Faulkner Theatre at the University of Mississippi and go to law school there and sweep off William Faulkner's grave every day.

Mark, the young narrator in *A Measure of Dust*, says that Huey Long "looked like a man made to live, to get all the kicks he could from life. I personally just never thought of a man like him dying." That's the way I viewed Steve.

His own measure of dust is somewhere in the Pacific now, mixing endlessly with the ghostly echo of the USS *Lexington's* mighty guns, and with the last spent breaths of his eternally youthful comrades, sleeping.

• • • 🐾 • • •

# The Michael DeBakey of Machinery

Stepfathers are commonplace nowadays, but when I was growing up I was the only kid in my neighborhood who had one. There was a stigma attached to stepparents in those days, and I tried to avoid the issue. I didn't want him coming around when he first started picking my mother up, so I put nails in the driveway to make him get a flat. Whether he got one or not I never knew, but I knew it didn't stop him. This may have explained why he didn't speak to me for about the first five years after they got married. He was never mean; he just ignored me.

But he gave me ten dollars once. This was when I was getting on the bus in Pampa to go back home to live with my grandparents in Cleburne. I didn't know whether it was because he liked me or because he was happy I was leaving. I took the money anyway.

At some point, though, he started talking to me and eventually got to where I couldn't stop him. We became best friends. But before that, he was a sphinx. He was a good-looking guy in those days, with broad shoulders and the look of an old-time cowboy star like Randolph Scott. He always had money and a nice car. I went with him one day in Pampa when he bought a new 1953 Mercury hard-top convertible. The salesman asked him how he would like to make the payments. Raymond said, "I'll make 'em all right now," and counted out thirty-two one hundred dollar bills.

I didn't know much about him for a long time except that his name was Raymond Basham and that he was a crane operator for Texas Steel Company in Fort Worth before being transferred to Pampa. And that he had been with the 36th Infantry Division in World War II and a prisoner of war in Stalag 4B in Germany. Maybe this POW experience made him so independent. He never took out a loan in his life or owned an insurance policy that wasn't required by law. After he died, several companies turned me down for insurance on his house because it had never been insured before. He bought clothes at the flea market and stuffed the pockets with hundred dollar bills. You would be surprised by the improvement $27,000 stuffed into the lapel pocket can make on the appearance of a polyester suit.

Other than holding onto money with great tenacity, Raymond's greatest skill was repairing things. He was the Michael DeBakey of machinery. His fine, steady fingers moved for a time over a clogged carburetor; tiny seals were inserted into tiny slots; floats set at precise levels; miniature screws replaced and tightened. Shortly, as if by magic, somebody's car was running like a Swiss watch.

He was the transplant champion of the machine world. Brushes bad on a generator? No problem. Just remove some good ones from the generator on an engine with a bad crankshaft or other fatal ailment and transplant them. A short circuit in the tail lights? No need to rewire. Just run a wire directly to the battery and to a switch on the dashboard to cut them off. Presto. Bypass surgery.

He could eyeball point gaps and other measurements to a thousandth of an inch. He could set a car's alignment with a straight cane pole, which he somehow used to set the toe-in and camber.

To those opting to spend not mend, Raymond wouldn't be accorded much status. His garage was a rubble of tools, buckets of parts, small motors, engines, transmissions, cigar boxes of light fixtures, breaker switches, gaskets, bearings. There were stacks of filters, unopened boxes of spark plugs, piles of alternators, springs, gears, starters, and compressors. Hundreds of pulley belts hung from nails. There were chain saws, hand saws, coping saws, and saw blades. Hammers of every size and function. Clamps, drills, drill bits, drill presses, dozens of boxes and jars of screws and nuts, lock washers and cotter pins, and a cast-iron steam engine. There was a full-size motor boat in there and a 1963 Volvo—both full of machinery.

Finally, his holdings became so extensive that he could no longer get inside the garage without squeezing his slender body between colossal mounds of parts. My mother used to say that she was afraid every time he went in there that she might not ever see him again. So most of the time, he just squatted on his haunches outside the door, tinkering with some new treasure to add to his impenetrable Fort Knox of junk.

He smoked Prince Albert and Bugler most of his life, and this killed him at the age of eighty-one. The doctors asked me if I wanted his lifeless body connected to a ventilator after his heart and kidneys had worn out. I said no. Raymond lived to keep machines alive—he wouldn't want it the other way around.

· · · 🦌 · · ·

## The Ghost of Christmas Future is Orange and Glows in the Dark

My wife's family has grown too large for us to celebrate Christmas with very much peace and good will. The women always try to invent new ways to avoid having to buy so many gifts, but these innovations usually cause turmoil such as you would expect to find on a game show. For the past few years, we've had "Let's Make a Deal" Christmases.

One year, someone came up with the bright idea of passing random gifts around among the family on Christmas Eve. If you didn't like the gift, you could pass it on, hoping for a better one on the next go-around. This plan evolved into the present strategy of numbering the gifts and then drawing for them. Everyone then opens them and holds the loot up to be assayed. If you like someone else's better than your own, you simply take it from them and leave yours in return. "Let's Make a Deal" has evolved into "Survival of the Fittest." Last year, a lifetime bond of affection was eroded by a dispute over a magnetic neon refrigerator ornament that lit up and played "We Three Kings."

This is the women's problem. Men have the problem of not knowing how to react when opening a gift from their mother-in-law. Men are less talented than women at hiding their true feelings. Women can make you believe that the repair kit for their window blinds is just the thing they've been combing the stores for. Men aren't born with the pretending-you-like-a-gift-that-you-really-abominate gene. Men stare down at the offending article and become mute. Sweat pours down. The brain is unable to formulate a ready lie. The nervous system shuts down; the tongue dries out and sticks to the roof of the mouth. Finally, when the system comes back up, the poor devil hears words tumbling stupidly from his lips. They are great ennobling words, though, whatever they may chance to be, for they have been purchased with the coin of immense suffering.

My brother-in-law and I once tried to send our mother-in-law a hint that she should cease and desist with the gifts like matching fuschia sport shirts. We wore them to a formal function that she was hosting. She loved it. Next year, she got us matching double-knit jump suits.

I guess my brother-in-law thought it called for more extreme tactics. The only thing was, I wasn't in on the plan. What he did the next Christmas was he gave me a pair of enormous orange work gloves that glowed in the dark. He signed the card, "From your mother-in-law."

I fell for it. I thought she had stepped over the line this time with this preposterous gift. I didn't care any more. I couldn't hold up the façade any longer.

Great massive shuddering pyroxisms of laughter took over my body. I laughed. I cried. I gagged. I rolled in the floor. "I can't say it!" I cried. "I can't say I like orange gloves that glow in the dark! I give up!"

I had met defeat. There was nothing to do but prostrate myself before the omnipotent mother-in-law goddess who alone understands the eternal divine wisdom of orange gloves that glow in the dark.

"Have you gone crazy?" I heard my wife saying through the fog. "Get up off the floor and act like a grown person. You're scaring the children. Besides, that's a gag gift from your goofy brother-in-law!"

Mother-in-law, however, was untouched by this outburst. If she got the point of my yuletide breakdown she didn't show it. "Why is he doing that?" she said.

Then, she moved happily toward the gloves. She picked them up and inspected them lovingly. "Do they really glow in the dark?" she said. "I wish I had thought of that. I wonder if they have shorts and shirts to match."

Terror seized me. I had seen the ghost of Christmas Future—and it was orange and glowed in the dark.

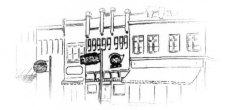

# 1993

*A small town is a place where every Old Man Warner
ought to feel content that the lottery is safe
from outside control.*

## Put it on Cooksey's Bill

When singer Ronnie Dawson was just a little chip off his daddy's bass fiddle, he lived in the countryside near Waxahachie. His father was a farmer and also had his own band, "Pinky Dawson and the Merrymakers." Ronnie walked part of the way home from school some days with a friend named Archy Cooksey. Archy's father had a charge account at a store they passed on the way. Ronnie watched in wonderment one day as Archy got a Coke and Baby Ruth and said, "Put it on Cooksey's bill!"

It was magic! Just say these words and get a free Coke and Baby Ruth!

"What's a bill?" Ronnie asked himself over and over in bed at night. He wondered whether he had one and just didn't know it.

"What's a bill, Dad?" he asked one day.

"A bill, son," his father said, "is the shade on a cap. It's the teeth of a bird. It's a man's name, a personal debt, or a senator's pet project."

This left him nowhere. None of these things added up to a Coke and a Baby Ruth. The matter called for action.

He stood in front of the mirror and practiced. "Put it on *Cooksey's* bill. Put it on Cooksey's *bill*." They both sounded wrong.

Eventually, the day came when he thought he had practiced enough. On the way home that day, he went into the store. The screen door banged shut behind him. He looked at the candy bars, so colorfully wrapped and lined up in rows so neat and straight. Hershey's. Fifth Avenue. Peanut Log. Snickers. Butterfinger. Baby Ruth. He liked them all—but would it work with the others?

He selected the Baby Ruth, then turned and lifted the lid on the cold drink box. He thrust his hand into the unbearably cold water and fished out a Coke. He shoved it under the cap-remover and popped it off. The cap dropped into the container. The thunk it made clarioned loud and clear that it was too late to call it off, the point of no return. His heart was pounding as it had when he was called on to say the prayer at Sunday school.

"Put it on Cookey's bill!" he told the proprietor.

The words rolled off his tongue like a Grand Ole Opry tune.

It worked that day, the next, and every day after that for a month. To him, these words ranked right up there with Shazam and Abracadabra for magical properties. Life is a mystery for a six-year-old boy, he thought, but a Coke and a Baby Ruth can go a long way toward clearing it up.

It was a Coke and Baby Ruth heaven for a whole month long.

But at the end of the month, he came home from school and saw Mr. Cooksey's car sitting in front of his house.

The bad thing about getting the whipping, Ronnie says today, is that he had to figure out on his own what he had done wrong. Even after the whipping, he still didn't know what a bill was. All he knew was that it was somehow wrong for him to say, "Put it on Cooksey's bill," and he wasn't going to do it anymore.

I wrote the lyrics and Ronnie wrote the melody to a song about this incident, and he sings it in his act sometimes. Audiences seem to like it but have varying opinions about its meaning. Some see it from a religious point of view; others associate it with the credit card epidemic, or even the national debt.

I never really thought about these things. If I were forced to explain this story, though, I would say that the meaning of right and wrong is not as clear and absolute as we wish it to be.

· · · ❦ · · ·

# Birthday Bard

Shakespeare is one of my heroes. Others include Elvis Presley and Roy Rogers. I especially like it when they come back from the dead, like Elvis. As far as I know, no English teacher ever reported seeing Shakespeare on a Piggly-Wiggly parking lot, but we all agree that what he did was pretty miraculous. With but a sixth-grade education, this poor glover's son managed to learn everything worth knowing about law, the military, courtly life, history, philosophy, philology, psychology, and foreign countries into which he had never set foot. He also had cosmic knowledge of human nature and wrote poetry that would make an angel swoon.

April twenty-third is his birthday. I sometimes acknowledge it by writing a sonnet, hoping he and I might "yoke together, like a double shadow," as he puts it so deftly, hoping that his power might somehow lift me to new literary heights, so that I might change the course of American letters, usher in the millennium, and end all wars.

Well, this hasn't happened. The reason may be, as I am now being told, is that I've been sucking my soliloquies from a contraband quill, drawing fire from counterfeit coals, rhyme from a mock muse. Oh the humanity! They say my Will is a bogus bard!

My prayers for the perfect pentameter haven't been answered because I've been petitioning a decoy deity, a fake, a swindle, an *ignis fatuus* of artifice.

Shakespeare's defunct.

This, you say, is nothing new. English teachers have battled these rumors for years. With these professors, God's existence may be a matter for debate but question the authorship of *Hamlet* and you'll be lucky to escape with all your body parts. But Hawthorne, it is said, secretly did not believe in the bard. Neither did Emerson, Whitman, and Mark Twain. We pity them in their ignorance.

And these heavily footnoted tomes by gownsmen like Greenwood, Looney, Ogburn, and a dozen others—challenging Shakespeare's authenticity? The Miss Grundys of the academic world consider this research to be only tabloid scholarship by Geraldos in a mortarboard.

Comes now, on Shakespeare's birthday, heavy bombardment in the form of scholarly articles in two conservative magazines. *Atlantic Monthly* and *National Review* have come out with more evidence against his authenticity. It is improbable, they say, that the world's greatest plays could have issued from the hand of this uneducated, small-Greek and Latin-reading, bit-acting, deer-poaching, money-lending son-of-a-glove-making ignoramus. Or something to that effect.

"Shakespeare" merely allowed himself to be a front for an Elizabethan author who needed anonymity, the magazines state. The real author must have been someone of royal birth, who had the education, breeding, and means to travel. This mystery poet, they say, is Edward De Vere, 17th Earl of Oxford.

Well, well. The snobs of the world strike again. They can't accept the notion that a poor kid from the boondocks of Stratford could write *Othello*. They had to come up with a fop like Edward De Vere, someone our Will would have laughed his guts out at.

What will the literary cops come up with next? Well, even if they find a smoking gun, or flaming quill, whatever, some irrefutable fact that proves Oxford really is Shakespeare, it won't matter. When fact clashes with myth, myth wins every time. As our Will rightly says:

*What custom wills, in all things should we do't,*
*The dust on antique time would lie unswept,*
*And mountainous error be too tightly heapt*
*For truth to o'er-peer.*

Next, I guess they'll try to make me believe that my Roy Rogers is just a city boy from Cincinnati named Leonard Slye.

## The Fender Skirt King of Texas

I wouldn't glance across the street to see the King of Pop, the King of England, or the Box Office King, whoever that might be at the moment. But I would certainly drive to Whitney to see the Fender Skirt King of Texas. Now, that's genuinely something to jump-start my car to see. Plus as it turned out, I needed a set of fender skirts. A 1951 Ford just doesn't look quite right without skirts.

So I called up my old pal Paul Benson, whose reverence for all things curious never flags. P. B. and I met at Dee-Tee's in Midlothian to drink coffee and plan our outing to fender skirt heaven.

The domain of Big Jim Tidwell is easily found on Highway 22 in Whitney and is worth the trip to satisfy all your fender skirt needs. His building warehouses over 6,000 pairs. They are everywhere, pile on top of pile, stacked and catalogued from floor to ceiling like documents in the Fender Skirt Library of Congress.

Want a pair of skirts for a 1941 Buick Roadmaster? One guy did, and he was willing to drive from Kansas and pay Big Jim $750 for them. Somebody else drove from Oregon for a pair to fit a 1942 De Soto.

I came after Ford skirts, and it just so happens that Big Jim likes Fords. Out back is old Ford paradise. There they are, Ford carcasses that in their day made their owner the envy of the neighborhood. Oh the passion once engendered in those rolled-and-pleated Naugahyde seats! They are no longer repositories of teenage love and heartbreak. They are jammed full of—you guessed it—fender skirts. Across the street in the driveway of Big Jim's house sits a 1967 Trailways bus that he rebuilt from the ground up. "Why a bus?" I blurt out, naïve as an altar boy.

"Fender skirts!" he says. What was I thinking? For a moment I visualized rows of seats for people to sit in on trips to see the Liberty Bell.

"No seats!" says the Fender Skirt King.

No matter what national or international crisis may be gripping the country, old dudes are going to be restoring the cars they got their first, uh, romance, in, Big Jim says. "And when they do," he goes on, "sooner or later, they come to me, Big Jim, for their fender skirts. I may be prejudiced, because I'm the Fender Skirt King, but I don't think there's anything that helps a car's looks any more than a pair of fender skirts."

Big Jim says he sells more skirts than all the other dealers in the country combined, sometimes $2,000 worth in a day. In the fender skirt bus, he travels around the country to swap meets, where he buys and sells skirts. But most of his sales are by mail order. He has sold skirts to customers in Australia, Japan, Brazil, South Africa, Canada, you name it. "I just box 'em up and mail 'em out!" he said.

"I can see you enjoy your work," I said to the King.

Before he could answer, a cellular phone rang from inside his pocket. It was Europe calling, I think. He jotted down some notes and hung up. "I've been doing this for six years," he said, getting back to me. "But before that I ran the convenience store next door. That almost drove me crazy. Now, there's nothing else in the world I'd rather be doing than selling a man a pair of skirts."

"Big Jim is lucky to be able to make a living doing what he loves," I said, as we tooled down the blue highway toward Midlothian. "If you can make a lot of money at it, then I guess that's even better, as long as the money doesn't become the passion."

"I didn't like it that he had a cell phone in his pocket," P. B. said. "It ruins it for the Fender Skirt King to have a cell phone."

I didn't want to think about that. Thanks to Big Jim, I had a new set of modified 1951 Mercury skirts that would make me the envy of all the old dudes down at Dee-Tee's.

Hoowee!

# Spitting Against the Wind of Change
## or
# The Town That Sprays Together
# Stays Together

Midlothian is at war with the American Civil Liberties Union. Some kid and his mother have filed suit against the school district for committing prayer somewhere in or around the curriculum, and the ACLU is involved.

As a result, Mr. and Mrs. Hoi Polloi of the town are inflicting a barrage of fiery letters on the local newspaper editor. Mr. and Mrs. Vox Populi, who tend to be more lenient, have yet to be heard.

One Mrs. Polloi wrote that she wasn't sympathetic to people who patronize these off-brand religions.

Another wrote that, "if these kids were promoting homosexual activities or drugs and abortion, these ACLU hoodlums would be hugging their necks. . . . We must stand behind our youth and school district and fight this Anti-Christ Legion of Un-American representations of Satan."

Well, it looks like the bottom has dropped out of the ACLU stock around here. What should anyone expect? A small town is a place where every Old Man Warner ought to feel content that the lottery is safe from outside control. We don't even talk in terms of civil liberties. We say "small town values." This means we work, go to church, pay our bills, and gossip about the ones who fail to do these things.

We also have a long tradition of praying at football games and pep rallies. We think God keeps an eye on the ball scores. I read in the local paper that someone suggested "lynching" this kid for jeopardizing our won-lost record. I didn't take this literally. I believe he would be given a fair trial first.

Also, I heard that some of the kids were spitting on the anti-prayer kid. They said they were "spitting for Jesus."

Now if this story is true, it could make us look bad among the more sophisticated city-dwellers. Personally I'm having an awfully hard time believing it, as spitting, for any reason, is strictly against the rules at Midlothian High School. If a kid even looked like he was going to spit, he would be in deep detention. He could say he was spitting for Troy Aikman, and it wouldn't make any difference.

I don't believe these prayerful students would let fly in clear violation of the rules. Prayerful students are obedient students. What probably happened was, they said to the anti-prayer kid, "Phooey on you!" and some expectorant, which is usually produced with the pronunciation of "phooey," showered onto him accidentally. You take a dozen or so kids, all saying "phooey" at the same time, and you've got the potential for some heavy dew.

But if by chance it did occur, I wouldn't be so quick to condemn it. There is a biblical precedent for spitting. Jesus himself was clearly pro-spitting and even warned his lukewarm followers: "I will spew you out of my mouth." And on another occasion, he is said to have spit into some dirt and made a paste and used it to heal a blind man's eyes. Knowing our biblical precedents is another of our small-town values.

Nevertheless, this whole thing has left me in a quandary. I'm a loyal small-townsman, but I just don't understand this issue. When did school kids get this overwhelming obsession with prayer? I always thought they liked to flirt and dance and drive their cars ninety miles an hour. When I was a school kid, every time we turned around, someone was trying to get us to pray. They threatened us. They even bribed us. "You want to go outside and smooch and drag race? Well, then, put your heads down and start praying. You might as well get it over with," they said, "because you're not going anywhere until you do! We'll be here all day if we have to."

Do the kids of today think there is a government plot to keep them from praying? If that's the case, maybe we should convince them that it's illegal to *read their books*.

· · · 🦂 · · ·

## Topping Out on the Ground Floor

My family isn't very happy right now, and it's not a very pleasant thing to see.

It's not my real family—it's my co-workers, but it's often called a family nowadays. We're having what you might call "domestic problems." I hate it.

Because of the dissolution of the traditional family, our co-workers have become "extended family." Many spend more time together than they do with real family. When this happens, the workplace takes on the dynamics of the traditional family. The boss is the parent; workers are sibling children. What happens next is inevitable, I am learning.

Sibling rivalry.

My co-workers and I are about the same age and have taught at the same Dallas community college together since 1970. At first we were young and had great fun. We had parties after class and on the weekends. We were filled with enthusiasm and hope. By the time we were fifty, we would certainly be college presidents of our own colleges, professors at prestigious universities, authors of great books. The world was our oyster.

Something funny just started happening. We're turning fifty and are still in the same offices, in the same classrooms, teaching children of students we taught years before.

It's not job offers from universities needing presidents and professors that we're receiving in the mail. Our mailboxes aren't stuffed with offers for book contracts from big publishers.

No, it's only AARP trying to get in touch with us.

This shouldn't be such a big deal. There's nothing wrong with having dreams and not achieving them. That's life. There's always another falling star to latch onto. What makes it bad is that so many people in the same workplace are going through the same midlife passage at the same time.

What happened to our dreams? Our nest was too comfortable, psychologists say, so we never spread our wings. Now, at fifty, we've "topped out." Since there is only so much territory to go around, we get hyper-competitive, fighting over turf. Get that bigger office, that telephone with the buttons that flash, extra-service contracts, R.C. Gorman prints for our walls—feather the nest. Only thing is—there are only so many feathers.

It's every bit as unpleasant as when real siblings fight. For me, anyway. I grew up with no brothers and sisters and never learned how to sible. The only other experience I've had with this phenomenon is when our children sibled. When they used to fight, my wife, who had sibling experience, shrugged it off. I hated it and tried to work it out for them. I'm trying to do the same thing with my collegial siblings, and the results are disastrous. They all hate the very fence I walk on.

Experts say we will eventually get along as before. Once you get through any kind of transition, you're okay.

Maybe that's the best analogy for this subject. It isn't easy realizing the world isn't your oyster after all. And even if it is, what do you do when you learn that, instead of a pearl inside, there's a kidney stone?

· · · 🍎 · · ·

# Moving Mama

When my stepfather died, I knew my mother wouldn't be able to stay in her house and live by herself. But she wanted to try, and I tried to help her make it work.

I called in the carpenters immediately and gave the house a complete makeover. Raymond had preferred keeping his money to modernizing the house, so I used some of it to bring it into the twentieth century.

Unfortunately, money couldn't restore her mind. I knew she was unable to care for herself, but she managed to stay there for almost a year because I enabled her to do it.

Every day after my classes and on weekends, I drove to Cleburne and took her out to eat, gave her her blood pressure pills, and took care of her bills. I washed her clothes, cleaned house, and screwed the light bulbs back in. At night, she took out all light bulbs and unplugged every appliance. She couldn't understand why her milk was spoiling.

I was slow to catch on. Her short-term memory has been failing for several years, as well as her other abilities. Raymond covered for her. Secretly, he had bought all the birthday and Christmas presents for the last few years. At mealtimes, he bought fast food. I thought he had just gotten tired of her cooking. Anyway, who cooks anymore? I thought little of it.

It has been a tough year. She has never lived alone before. She has never paid a bill or gone grocery shopping by herself. I tried to show her how to do these things, but it was hopeless. She bought the same things over and over and paid the same bill several times. I counted seventeen bottles of cooking oil in her kitchen and fourteen pounds of margarine—very soft margarine. The woman at the cable company said she was paid up there until the twenty-first century.

Last Christmas, I helped her put money into cards for the grandchildren. I knew she would forget so I kept them and put them under our Christmas tree. On Christmas Eve, she pulled out more cash and gave it to them. They just put it back into her purse rather than tell her what she had done. She's embarrassed about her forgetfulness.

On May 15 we drove to Fort Worth to pick up Raymond's insurance check. Then we went to her bank and deposited it.

She called every day for weeks and told me there was a check up at Fort Worth and we must go get it.

I spent a lot of time telling her that we had already done that. "Okay," she said, "I'll just get somebody else to take me." I even had the company write and tell her. I got a photocopy of the check and the deposit slip and showed them to her. Then I made six more copies and placed them in prominent places in the house and in the car. She called the next day and said, "There's a check at Fort Worth, and we have to go and get it."

I gave up. So she got her cousin Irene Qualls and her son Buck to take her to get the nonexistent check.

Everybody had been telling me to stop her from driving. I resisted. One day, I went to her house and found her in a state of nervousness. "What happened?" I said.

"Nothing."

"I know something happened."

"That old girl hit me."

"You had a wreck?"

"Yes, but it was her fault."

"Did you get a ticket?"

"No, but she did."

I looked in her purse and found two citations—one for running a red light and another for no insurance. She had an insurance card, but she evidently hadn't known how to show it to the officer. "You're right. You didn't get a ticket," I said. "You got two tickets."

After that, on January 13, she disappeared. We were afraid she was dead. The police found her at three in the morning in Glen Rose, twenty-five miles away.

It was clear at long last. I had to do something.

I found a nice facility with supervision between Midlothian and Cleburne. I told her it would be a new beginning.

My children stayed with her on that last night to give her support and help her pack. When they were little, they spent just about every weekend at her house.

The three of them came by my house on the way. Karen, who is thirty, said, "Here we go, to spend the night in that house together for the last time."

This is one of the things for which there should never be a last time.

· · · ❦ · · ·

## Horned Toads and Politicians

I guess I've lived in suburbia so long that I failed to note the passing of an old childhood friend, the friendly little "horny toad." I was reminded of this recently when I read *O Ye Legendary Horned Frog*, a new book by June Welch, the University of Dallas history professor, radio personality, author, and observer of all things Texan.

I used to see the critters everywhere when I was a kid. I liked to put them in my pocket and carry them to the nearest red ant bed. All you had to do was set Mr. Horny Toad on the mound and wait for the action. It was like watching my brother-in-law at the family reunion buffet table.

No one knows for sure what happened to the horned frog, writes Welch, but experts think it may be a result of the poison we use to kill fire ants. The poison is killing off the red ants, too, which were the horned toads' food supply.

This got me to thinking. Would this be like what might happen to politicians if taxes were suddenly removed from the legislative landscape? Everybody would be going around saying, "You know, I just thought of something. I haven't seen a politician in twenty years. Used to, every time you turned around, one of those devils was running for some kind of office. I kind of miss the sonuvaguns."

If taxes ever dried up, would politicians become extinct? After reading this book, I'm amazed at all the other similarities.

Horned frogs were seen only in late spring and summer, the book says, and went into hibernation from September or October to early May. When is Congress in session?

"The toad's main protection," Welch writes, "is blending into the background." Have you ever noticed how politicians can make themselves invisible as the first scent of controversy reaches their nostrils?

"In case of discovery, a horny toad makes a serious effort to intimidate the enemy," Welch goes on. "The creature can inflate itself to twice its normal size and appears to be dangerous." I've seen politicians swell up like this and bluster about the liberal media when they get caught paying for personal trips with tax money.

Also when agitated, "the toad flattens its body and can shoot a stream of blood a distance of three feet as an eyelid ruptures under pressure." I admit I've never seen a politician do this, but Dan Quayle seemed to implode and his eyes to get awfully red that time when Lloyd Bentsen told him he was no Jack Kennedy.

The horned toad's first chore each morning, the book says, is to raise its head out of the sand and "heat its blood." I can't bear to speculate on how Bill Clinton does this.

The horned toad's favorite mating technique, we are told, is to impress females by doing pushups. I read somewhere that Ted Kennedy stripped to his boxer shorts and did this when he was introduced to that pretty girl down in Florida. Or was that Strom Thurmond? I can't remember.

Another similarity is their resilience. The book's central anecdote is the story of "Old Rip," the horned toad said to have lived thirty-one years inside the cornerstone of the Eastland County courthouse. That's nothing. I heard there was a road commissioner in Hillsboro who had been in office so long they had to burn the courthouse down to get him out.

I guess politicians are here to stay, though, despite the similarities. It's too bad it had to be the horned toads to go instead of them.

· · · ❦ · · ·

## Classical Bones

A plain but attractive woman is bored with her life on the farm. Her husband is kind to her and prosperous but too busy with his farm work to notice that she is sexually unsatisfied. So she longs for adventure as she piddles in her flower garden.

An interesting craftsman stops by her farmhouse when her husband is away. Flowers get involved, then emotions. He hints that she should leave with him and join his life of adventure. She agonizes. Her heart is broken, but she stays with her husband on the farm.

This is certainly the plot of a hysterically renowned novel by new Texan Robert James Waller.

Well, it may sound like *The Bridges of Madison County*, but it is the story line of "The Chrysanthemums," a short story by John Steinbeck, written in 1933. In Steinbeck's era, sex could only be implied, so he had to rely on imaginative language and Freudian symbols to convey it. In other words, the sex was represented in the woman's subconscious mind by the flowers. In those days, a lot of literary sex took place like that.

In "The Chrysanthemums," the craftsman is a peddler instead of a photographer. He mends Elise's pots and pans, and she gives him flowers. Steinbeck's repressed wife has no children, and her fantasy lover wears soiled clothes and needs a manicure. There are other differences between the two works, but they are filler. The basic stories are the same.

If Steinbeck were alive, he wouldn't sue Waller. He would just fob it off and keep on drinking. He knew that writers like to unearth classical bones and flesh them out for their own stories.

*Pretty Woman* is a knockoff of *My Fair Lady*, which itself was a rip-off of *Pygmalion*, a story George Bernard Shaw cribbed from a Greek myth.

*West Side Story* is a retelling of *Romeo and Juliet*. This motif was also used as the basis for the 1940s film *Rosanna McCoy*. All three are rip-offs of *Pyramus and Thisbe*, another Greek myth.

Again, there's a tradition for literary thievery among even the best writers. Shakespeare, Chaucer, and Coleridge plagiarized openly. Sophocles took the story for "Oedipus Rex" from Book Eleven of *The Odyssey*. In modern times, Eugene O'Neill changed Agamemnon's name to General Mannon and the Trojan War to the Civil War and called his trilogy *Mourning Becomes Electra*. James Joyce brought the story of Ulysses to Dublin and didn't bother to change the name. Steinbeck himself transplanted Camelot to Monterey and called his book *Tortilla Flat*. Like Joyce and O'Neill, he sinned bravely and admitted his debt. No big deal. When great writers do it, it's called "homage."

So, why blame Waller? I only wish I had thought of it. All this gave me the idea to rewrite Steinbeck's *The Short Reign of Pippin IV* as a screenplay and transplant the setting from Paris to Washington. Then, I realized it had already been done.

It's called *Dave*.

· · · 🐚 · · ·

# The General and the Teenage Queens

As teenagers, my wife and her sister Betty were fond of young Freddy McFarren and gave him a thrill every now and then when they passed by his house in their short-shorts. Brenda and Betty were heart-stoppers and got married young and raised families.

Freddie turned his attention to books and got an appointment to West Point after his graduation from Cleburne High School in 1962.

Betty's younger son Robert Russell grew up and joined the Army, got into the 82nd Airborne, and fought in the Persian Gulf War. Freddy, now General Fred McFarren, also fought in that war.

Robert was stationed at Fort Bragg, North Carolina, after the war, as was General McFarren. When Robert got married, we all went to Fort Bragg for the wedding.

Soon after we got there, Brenda said, "I've got a bright idea. Let's call up Freddy and invite him to the wedding!"

Betty thought this idea was ever so nifty, adding the suggestion that he should also be invited to the dinner that evening. Then, they set about to look him up in the telephone book.

Robert, who looks like a youthful Major Dad, is a fearless paratrooper with frontline war experience, but when he heard this plan, he suddenly grew pale and his legs turned to mashed potatoes. "You don't just call up the general and ask him to dinner!" said this intrepid warrior who had jumped from high-flying planes on the field of battle. "As a matter of fact, you don't ask a general anything! Why, why, there's the chain of command. And there's protocol! Even a colonel doesn't just call up a general! Why, why—"

The mother and aunt looked at him blandly. "I can't wait to meet his wife," said Brenda. "We can tell her what a cute little boy he was."

"Oh the horror!" Robert said.

"Freddy's one of the sweetest little boys you ever saw, Robert," Betty said, consolingly. "He'll love it."

General McFarren was, in fact, happy to hear from his friends from the old neighborhood and showed up at the groom's dinner with his lovely wife, also from Cleburne. And he came as Freddy, in his civilian clothes, just like everybody else. No one could have been more genuinely gracious. He went around the room and spoke with the families and even made Robert feel as easeful as possible. He patted him on the back and congratulated him and wished him and the bride all the best.

Two days later he and his wife showed up at the little chapel on the base for the wedding. He wore his resplendent dress blues and all his ribbons and regalia. This time he was General McFarren, rigidly viewing the military formalities of the ceremony. But it was Freddy again after the ceremony, chatting amiably with these sisters who had thought nothing of calling him up and inviting him to an important family function. He seemed honored to be asked and maybe even moved by the experience.

In my cynicism, I was surprised that he came. That he showed up, not just for the dinner but also for the wedding of an enlisted man he had never even met, to accommodate two neighborhood girls from his long-ago small-town childhood, displays, I think, a quality that issues from a kind of neighborhood bonding that you don't see much anymore.

"The childhood shows the man as morning shows the day."

## Ain't Is to Die For

What's the big deal? So *Webster's Tenth Collegiate Dictionary* includes "ain't" without a warning label. Some people are bothered by this. I say it doesn't matter. Nothing is going to change the way people feel about this word. No student in my entire teaching career has ever written this word in a theme. Though I never told them they couldn't, not one ever did it—and I estimate I've read over 30,000 themes in my day.

They write every other crazy thing, though. One of their favorite occupations is putting apostrophes where they don't belong and leaving them out where they need to be. They love to use "lead" when they mean "led." They will never put a title on a theme, not ever.

The word the dictionary-makers should make legal is "alot." Forget about trying to preserve it as two words; let it be "alot" and be done with it. The same with "alright." These are students' favorite words. "I play Nintendo a lot, alright." "I watch *Doogie Howser* alot, alright." Students are going to do this and nothing can change it.

On the other hand, dictionary-makers can make "ain't" legal and offer a prize to the students who use it most and it won't matter. Students won't go near the word. You could spend hours, weeks, persuading them of its linguistic authenticity, charting its etymological evolution. You could tell them that Plato said it. Aristotle said it. Jesus said it. General by god Sherman said it. But I guarantee you that not even a grammaticized piece of the old *Tenth Collegiate Dictionary* in the back of the head would persuade them to write it.

Ain't is something you say in private, with only those you trust. It's never written down for a teacher to read. It has become a social taboo, etched in the lining of our genetic instruction sheet, implanted in our collective unconscious. I'm not sure how this happened. Sometimes, though, I think I have a brief recollection of being born. Doctors and nurses are hovering over me. They are chanting some kind of incantation. I think it is, "Never say ain't! Never say ain't!"

Nevertheless, it proves that, if everyone cooperates, anything can be taught.

I'm sure that no kid has ever written ain't in a theme, but I do recall one actually saying it in class. It was in my second grade class at Santa Fe Elementary School in Cleburne. Somebody had taken a Lone Ranger pedometer away from a boy named Alfred Sullivan. Our teacher, Miss Mary Spell, asked all the boys who had the pedometer. When she got to Albie Vandergriff, he said, "I ain't got it, Miss Spell."

A funeral pall settled over the classroom. Tiny bodies stiffened in their chairs, as if frozen. No one breathed. The chalkboards seemed to close in on us. Twenty tiny hearts thumped as one. I may have wet my homemade overalls.

"What did you say?" Miss Spell said.

"I said, 'I don't have it, Miss Spell,'" said the doomed child.

"That's not what you said the first time," she said, her inflections as cold as lime sherbet.

That child died mysteriously not too long after that. Though no one ever said so, my classmates probably believed, as I did, that saying ain't to an English teacher is what killed him.

· · · 🍎 · · ·

# A Seasoning of Life

Literary journals appeal to me in my dotage, as reading them is a lot like flicking around among the television channels. Another good analogy for a journal is the cafeteria. In fact, a literary journal is better than a cafeteria because you can sample all the entries before you have to consume them. First bite not so delicious, try another dish.

For journal enthusiasts, *Words From a Wide Land*, the new book from the hand of William Barney, is tasty all the way through. A poet's observations are more interesting than those of ordinary humans, and Barney is one of our best poets. He's the Robert Frost of Texas, has even won the Robert Frost Award. Fans of his poems will see the origins of many of them in this book. It's his eighth book and his first from the University of North Texas Press.

His subject is the joy and terror of life in all its forms, 365 entries gathered from over fifty years and stitched together in a colorful patchwork year of days. He is a naturalist and therefore a friend of flower, ant, bird, lizard, snake, potato plant, potato bug, and every other living thing that inhabits this earth, even people. There are occasional forays into locales other than Texas, including one glimpse into his meeting with Frost at the Hotel Astor in New York the time Frost gave him his award. But he is best when recording the teeming life of his own backyard in the Riverside area of Fort Worth.

It is the greatest drama of them all, the struggle for life within nature, death, and resurrection. This drama has five acts—spring, summer, fall, winter, and spring again. In Barney's drama, all things have consciousness. The cottonwood tree was a friend that he had to sacrifice when its branches became a threat to his roof. Two weeks later, April 6, 1983, he observed that buds had opened on the branches he had cut and stacked for waste. "They persist," he wrote, "in the hope for life even after the fatal cuts have been given."

There is humor. On November 14, 1973, he playfully suggested to his five-year-old granddaughter that they glue the falling leaves back onto the trees. To humor grandfather, she goes along with this game to the point of getting the glue. Finally, the game over, he wrote, "we sat in the swing in resignation and watched the stream of dead foliage, great heart-shaped ghosts, continue to fall."

Reading this book, I enjoyed learning what Barney was doing on special days in my life, or just what the weather was like. On my birthday in 1966, it was a foggy morning in Fort Worth after a cold night. He observed some turkey buzzards flying low in order to see food through the fog.

Well, hmmm, turkey buzzards on my birthday. Maybe it was eagles.

On January 20, 1961, Kennedy gave his stirring inaugural address, filling most citizens with hope. Barney's entry for that day concerns a dead starling on his windowsill.

*Words From a Wide Land* is a literary how-to book on living the good life. It's also a rare thing of beauty in a world that concentrates more and more on the ugly.

· · ·  · · ·

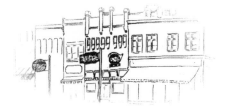

# 1994

*I would despair to learn that a family of line
dancers had moved into my neighborhood*

## Better to Reign in Hell Than
## Need a Car Part

Until recently, I had made great progress in overcoming my fear of auto parts salesmen. In the old days they were fearsome Darwinian throwbacks, usually glowering at you from behind their oil-stained counter, piled high with abandoned crankshafts, oil pans, camshafts, and oil pumps. Acrid clouds of cigarette smoke hung in the air. There would be a mangy dog somewhere.

Now, they look like regular people, and the stores are clean, modernized, and computerized. But something is wrong. As unpleasant as it was back in the old days to go in and buy a part, at least it was usually the right part. In the past few years, I've observed that while the stores and the salesmen look better, they nevertheless seem creepy and demonic underneath. They have the aspect of the ancient trickster about them.

I first noticed this a couple of years ago when I went into such a place located between Midlothian and Cedar Hill to buy a radiator core for a 1970 Plymouth Barracuda. This seemed a simple enough transaction, so I hadn't brought the old one with me for comparison before I paid for it. Of course, the one they sold me didn't fit. "You told me you wanted a radiator core for a 1979 Mustang," the trickster said when I returned it.

As time has passed, this pattern has gotten worse. Go in, tell these tricksters exactly which part you want. Get home—wrong part!

Finally, I tried ordering through a parts house catalogue. At least I wouldn't have to endure the rolling of the irritated parts house salesman's eyes and the threatening sibilant noises he makes when he has to restock the wrong part and search out another possibility. The catalogue would be easy. Fill out the order form: set of piston rings for a 1979 Nisson 280-ZX. Sit back and wait for the parts to appear in my mailbox. No fear. No intimidation. No hassle. Ain't life great!

The package shows up one fine day with the parts. Open it up. Not rings. No, not rings at all.

It's a *motorcycle helmet*.

I've had many such frustrations trying to keep the bondo-express fleet on the road, but I've just recently had another attack of my *autopartssalesmanophobia*. One of the characteristics of this malady is that you associate auto parts stores with the stygian depths of Hades. But this particular experience took me to car parts hell.

It is a Nisson dealership in suburban Dallas. The parts salesmen there wear people masks, but they are really Beelzebub, Lucifer, and the Beast of the Apocalypse. "I need an oil pressure sender unit, a door lock assembly, a headlight switch assembly, and a front wheel bearing and locknut for a 1985 Nisson four-wheel-drive pickup," I say, as authoritatively as I can, "manufacture date, 1-'85." I was proud of myself. Show the slightest sign of fear or uncertainty in a parts store, and you're doomed. You'll be hissed at and passed over for another victim. I hadn't stuttered or hesitated. I had memorized my lines and practiced them during the drive.

Beelzebub wasn't impressed. He glared at me, his eyes reflecting the lake of fire. "We'll have to order all that," he said. "Check back day after tomorrow."

"By the way," I make bold to inquire, "how much on that light switch?"

His eyes redden and his tail twitches threateningly as he searches through the computer files of parts hell. "That'll be $66.60," he says, "for a switch like that."

"Isn't that a little steep?" I say, stupidly.

"Nobody's begging you to buy it," says Beelzebub. I thought I saw him grin fiendishly at Lucifer and Beast as I hurried away, partless.

Time comes, I drive in for my parts. "Not in yet," says Beelzebub.

"Why not?" I manage to utter. "Today is the day after tomorrow."

Lucifer adjusts his horns for conflict. "Computers are down. Sorry. Check back next week."

After two more trips, I finally get the parts.

I had overcome the forces of auto parts hell and lived to tell the story.

Not quite. Remember the $66 light switch? Well, it was the wrong one.

Again, I approach the lake of fire to return it, this time bearing the old switch. "I'd appreciate it if you could sell me a new one just exactly like this old one," I say. "The one you sold me before was, uh, wrong."

I had hesitated. It was a sign of weakness.

Beelzebub and Lucifer glare at the offending part, then at me. I feel my skin blanching. Lucifer, who is the boss, naturally takes over at this point and brings out another switch. It matches the old one. "That'll be thirty dollars more," Lucifer says.

"Thirty dollars more!" I say. "What gives? First, you sell me the wrong part. Then you trot out the right one and say it's thirty dollars more."

I would live to regret this insolence.

The three demons looked knowingly at one another as if to say, "You want the right part, you gotta pay for the right part!"

Well, what's thirty bucks, I say to myself. At least, it's all over. I have overcome the forces of darkness. Yet, as I departed, I thought I heard an eerie voice saying, "You'll be back! Ha Ha Ha Ha Ha Ha!"

Back home. Get the switch installed on the truck. Door latch, oil pressure sending unit—everything works. The only thing left is the wheel bearing.

But where is it? It's not in the box. It's nowhere.

I recall the ominous warning as I departed Lucifer's pit. I call on the telephone. Beast answers. From this conversation I learn that, for wreaking sheer torture, Beast makes his fellow demons seem like cherubs from pansy heaven.

"I'll have to order that," he says. "Have it for you Thursday. Ha Ha Ha Ha Ha!"

On Thursday I call, just to make sure the part is in before I drive the fifteen miles to get it. Again, Beast answers. "Sure," he says, "it's here. No problem. Ha Ha Ha Ha!"

I stride confidently through the glass gates of hell. It's Beelzebub this time, hunched over the parts monitor, his horns protruding through the mesh of his good old boy cap. "Hep ye?" Beelzebub says.

"I've come for my bearing," I say, as naïve as an altar boy.

Demonically, he begins pounding away at his keyboard. "No, you don't understand," I say, "it has already been ordered. It's here. Where's Beast? He said he was holding it for me."

Beast appears in a puff of exhaust smoke. "Sorry," Beast says. "Somebody sold that bearing about an hour ago. It's gone."

"But, but, you were holding it for me," I mutter.

"Sorry," says Beast. "It was a glitch in the system. Want me to order another one for you? It'll be here next week."

"I don't get it," I say, brassily. "How to explain this sudden demand in Dallas for a left front wheel bearing for a 1985 Nisson truck?"

"I couldn't say, pal," Beast says, idly cleaning the countertop with his tail.

"I'd like to speak with Lucifer," I say.

He appears. "Lucifer," I say, "Beast says the wheel bearing he was holding for me has been sold. I can't believe this. Does it make any sense that somebody would sell it, after I was assured by Beast that he was holding it for me?"

"No," said this marble-hearted fiend. "It makes no sense at all. It's a glitch in the system."

"Ha Ha Ha Ha Ha Ha!" cackle his odious under-fiends.

So there's only one hope of ever getting my wheel bearing, I thought, as I drove back to the planet earth.

Back home, I dig out my parts catalogue and begin filling out the order form.

"Please send one *motorcycle helmet*," I write.

· · · 🐛 · · ·

# The Great Midlothian Sawdust War

Here in Midlothian, we have a good town squabble every so often. This time, though, it doesn't involve those pointy-headed intellectuals with chemistry degrees who drive into town and interfere with the business of our number one employer, Texas Industries.

This time it was regular people, and the fight wasn't about hazardous waste-burning. It was about—*sawdust.*

A local businessman wanted to change the zoning laws so that he could place a sawdust-transfer facility on his property downtown where the lumberyard used to be. All the regular people got the fantods over this. You would think that the hazardous-waste smoke billowing out of the stacks nearby would warrant a tad more concern than a couple of truckloads of woodchips a day. But we don't really understand things like chemical compounds and ozone layers. Woodchips we know. It's ever so much easier to get nasty at each other over something simple.

Plus, zoning laws were involved. Who doesn't want to protect their property value? I would despair to learn that a family of line dancers had moved into my neighborhood. So, to keep out bootscooters, I generally support the committee that divides the town into such zones as residential, commercial, industrial, and light and heavy bootscootin'. I could understand both sides.

So the town went to war with Jerry Spillers, the man who would be sawdust king. Angry letters to the *Midlothian Mirror* opposed the sawdust. Over three hundred regular people signed a petition against it. Dozens of trucks, maybe hundreds, would be hauling this stuff in, they cried. Like the dinosaurs, we would be choked out of existence. It would mean the end of Midlothian as we know it.

The protesters, I mean regular people, won and the man who would be sawdust king dropped the issue.

In any case, Midlothian is still a sawdust-free environment. Jerry took me downtown and showed me what he had planned to do. The trucks would have backed into an airtight facility where the sawdust and woodchips from a Duncanville cabinet factory would have been sucked into a boxcar, then transported to New Mexico for recycling into particleboard. He believed it would have been safe and environmentally sound.

He was the man who helped me settle in this town. He was the first person I met when I came here twenty-three years ago with a wife and three children, no money, and nowhere to live. "I have a job," I told him, "as a schoolteacher."

"I believe in schoolteachers," he said, and sold us a nice house and carried the note for the down payment (creative small-town bookwork).

He started buying real estate in this town when a lot of people were still betting on the future of cotton. He says he doesn't know anything about stocks, mutual funds, or the international oil cartel; he just believed in this town and invested in its future. Why, he asked, would he do anything to hurt it?

He pointed to a large metal building on the other side of the railroad tracks. "That's the same operation except it's a sodium product," he said. "Nobody has ever said a word about that."

So what do you intend to put on the property now?" I say.

"Nothing controversial this time. Just an Exxon station."

# Grocery Values

Going to the grocery store was an experience to look forward to in the days before big supermarkets and convenience stores. The small, family-owned grocery stores of those days are virtually extinct in the modern world.

There were a lot of them in Cleburne when I was growing up. They were lush with the fragrance of ground coffee, fresh vegetables, and yeasty bread. You could smell this for blocks because there was no air conditioning and the doors would be open. Grocery stores then were different from today's impersonal, antiseptic supermarkets with their ubiquitous generic, piped-in music; steroid-and-red-dye-injected, cellophane-encased meat; chemicalized fruit and vegetables, void of all taste and smell; and disengaged check-out girls and sack boys, their brains gone slack from the ceaseless chirp of the computerized scanners. "Paper or plastic?" "You have a work number?" "Have a nice day."

We walked to town every Saturday afternoon to get groceries, always early enough so that my grandparents could get back home in time to listen to the Grand Ole Opry. Going west across the Henderson Street Bridge, the first grocery store we came to was Burd's Grocery. This was our favorite, along with Given's on the south side of town, about an hour's walk from our house. To get all the way to Given's, we passed not only Burd's but also Parkway, Wofford's, Dempwolf's, Person's, Cash Service, Safeway, Wiggins', and Ball's. We went there because, during the Depression, R.E. Given let my grandfather have groceries on credit though he had no money to pay. When he went to work for the Santa Fe Railroad, he paid his bill and kept up his regular visits, but on a cash basis, throughout his life. Either Mr. Given or his son Charles always brought us home in a car. Other times, though, we stopped at Burd's.

Ted Burd, a stubby man with an ever-present cigar in the side of his mouth, seemed always to be hurrying up and down the aisles from his office to the meat counter and back again. His office at the front of the store had a large, cluttered roll-top desk and a portrait of President Roosevelt on the wall.

Behind the meat counter, Bill Randolph, the butcher, sawed, sliced, and chopped the meat like a madman. He was a one-man rendering plant. He had crooked, arthritic hands, and always a cigar stub burned in his mouth. Ashes floated down into the meat, mixing with the sweat coursing from his forehead and meat spatterings dribbling down from his chin to season the packinghouse-fresh, non-steroid-and-red-dye-injected, butcher-paper-wrapped-and twine-tied-USDA-grade-A roasts and steaks.

The store nearest to our house was Crow Grocery, a small, neighborhood grocery owned and operated by the Crow brothers, Burnice and Charley. (They had a cut-out of a crow on the front of the store as a logo. I don't think Burd's played on its own fowlish metaphor.) Burnice sketched portraits of movie stars and clipped them to a wire strung across the ceiling. I always looked to see if Rhonda Fleming and Lana Turner were still there before fishing a Mission Orange out of the unbelievably cold water of the drink box. Across the aisle in the bread and pastry rack, Coconut Snowballs, chocolate-filled cupcakes, Devil Dogs, fried pies, and cinnamon rolls seemed to sing out to me like ancient sea goddesses. The beautiful candy bars, stacked neatly in rows, waited at the front counter. If, somehow, I made it past the pastries, I was virtually helpless to resist the candy. I viewed candy in those days as one of the seven basic food groups.

My favorite time to go there was in the evening with my grandfather to get his Prince Albert and socialize with his friends from the neighborhood. They smoked and talked about the railroad and departed friends and how hard life had been in the

Depression. There was never any talk about sports or celebrity trash. The only famous people they cared about were those on the Grand Ole Opry and politicians.

They were more than grocery stores back then. The owners lived in the town, sometimes in the neighborhood, and you could get groceries on credit if you needed to, without a credit card—and they would bring the groceries to your house if you couldn't get to the store.

They were places to meet and talk with your friends. Today, grocery stores are designed to be impersonal, with the emphasis on rushing in and rushing out, with "Have a nice day!" as your only communication with another human being.

It seems not to matter to anyone. If they want to talk, they call in to a talk show.

$$\bullet \ \ \bullet \ \ \bullet \ \ \text{❦} \ \ \bullet \ \ \bullet \ \ \bullet$$

## What Would Gordon Do

The baseball strike has left fans with a void, but there used to be a stoppage every week. This was before air travel, and the teams needed Mondays off for traveling long distances by train. But these weekly hiatuses didn't silence Gordon McLendon, the most dramatic and eloquent of baseball announcers. No game on Monday? No problem. The Old Scotsman, as he was known, simply reached back into his files of the *Sporting News*, chose a classic game, and "re-created" it for his listeners using only the box scores and his lyrical imagination.

I heard the game in which Johnny Vander Meer pitched his second consecutive no-hitter on June 15, 1938. Also, the game of May 2, 1917 when Fred Toney and Hippo Vaughn pitched a no-hit game against each other. Through the Old Scotsman's unique brand of time-travel baseball, I felt I was actually hearing these games live. In fact, Toney himself heard the game, the Old Scotsman told me. Toney was driving his pickup, dialing his radio, when the game came on. He had been out of baseball for years. He was elderly and unfamiliar with re-creation techniques. He couldn't understand why that game was going on. He thought he had lost his mind. It upset him so that he wrecked his truck. McLendon said he heard about it and paid to have his truck repaired.

On the other six days, the Old Scotsman, along with sidekick Wes Wise, sat in his KLIF studio in the Oak Cliff section of Dallas and broadcast the major league games on his Liberty Network of 456 affiliates nationwide. He simply positioned an employee with binoculars and a telephone on top of a building adjacent to the stadium, took the information the employee gave him, and turned it into baseball drama. Other times he received the play-by-play, a few innings late, off the ticker tape machine.

Red Barber originated re-creations, but McLendon perfected them by adding sound effects and color commentary. A bat suspended overhead and tapped with a pencil sounded like a batted ball. Slapping a pillow represented the sound of the pitched ball hitting the catcher's mitt. For crowd noises, he used taped sounds from the major league stadiums. The hecklers at Fenway had Boston accents.

His re-creations became so popular that fans started staying home and listening rather than buying tickets. Attendance dropped dramatically, and club owners banded together after the 1951 season and got an injunction, preventing him from broadcasting in their territory. The Old Scotsman's baseball days were over and his network destroyed.

I've thought about how he would have filled the void of this strike if he were here today. Would today's fans, benighted as many are said to be of baseball history, care about the exploits of Tris Speaker, Frankie Frisch, or even Bobby Thompson?

I brought out my tape of the game in which Thompson hit the famous home run, the "shot heard 'round the world," and listened to it on the anniversary of that game, October 3, 1951. I know it almost by heart, but I never get tired of hearing the Old Scotsman's dramatic inflections and imaginative language. A winning pitcher was "serving the death warrant" in a game that was "tighter than seven sardines in a size-six can." When an underdog team was winning away from home, it was "bearding the lion in its den." A slugger was a "big siege gun in the arsenal." A team didn't just make a comeback—it "showed a heart of oak" as it "returned from the death agony," "fought the final summons," or "came back from the pale." Umpires didn't merely get angry—they got "mad as a flock of pelicans with lockjaw," and managers "hopped around like floorwalkers in Macy's basement."

And if he were around today he might also say, sadly, that baseball itself is "fighting the final summons," because greed "is serving the death warrant."

· · · 🐛 · · ·

## The Double-Dog Days of August

August meant grape-picking weather—and the divine fact of my grandmother's grape jelly.

My grandmother would put on one of my granddaddy's long-sleeved shirts, thick stockings, gloves, and bonnet—her poison-ivy proof outfit—and we would fetch our baskets and head for where the wild vine grows.

Kids nowadays have Disney World and Six Flags and lots of other exciting commercial activities, but I grew up in an era before organized fun.

To get to the grapes, we had to crawl through a fence and follow Buffalo Creek for a long way until it widened into a swimming hole deep in the woods, northeast of Cleburne. The older boys called this place "Grapey" because high trees formed a canopy over it, and they were full of grapevines. These boys swung on the vines and dropped into the water.

The swimming hole was usually full on these hot August afternoons. I wasn't allowed to go in because I hadn't learned how to swim. But one day as we were picking grapes nearby, I could hear the boys splashing in the water. I begged her until she said I could go over and watch. I wouldn't go in, I promised.

I left her to fill the baskets and ran through the vines to where they were swimming. They were all very old—thirteen, maybe older. It was so hot, and the water was so cool. Maybe I could have kept my promise if they hadn't started double-dog daring me. I had no idea when I made that promise that double-dog dares were going to get involved.

Soon, my clothes lay in a pile on the bank and I was swinging through the air on a vine high over the water. I was Tarzan, high in the jungle. The other boys were treading water below, yelling for me, Man of the Jungle, to turn loose.

I felt my foot scrape the edge of the bank before I hit the water. A neighborhood boy, Bill Leonard, pulled me out. I had cut my foot on a sharp rock and laid the soft flesh open to the bone.

They helped me get my clothes on and went to get my grandmother. She tore a piece off the bottom of her shirt and wrapped my foot to stop the bleeding. It was a long way back home, but the boys took turns carrying me and the baskets of grapes. My foot hurt but not so much as my conscience for going back on my promise.

When we got back home, she went out to the shed and brought back a fruit jar of kerosene, which she called "coal oil," and used it to wash out the wound. My friends watched, wide-eyed, each telling the story later with his own fantastic version of the adventure.

The next morning, I looked out of my bedroom window and saw smoke coming from beneath the iron kettle. I knew this meant she was cooking the grapes. When they were ready, she dipped out the mixture and separated the pulp by squeezing it all through cheesecloth. Then, she cooked it some more and added about five pounds of sugar and something else that made it thicken. It all seemed magical.

Before long, we had about two dozen jars of delicious grape jelly. My foot throbbed but I didn't care. I knew that hot biscuits packed with my grandmother's mustang grape jelly could take your mind off just about anything.

Kids today say it's hard to please their parents in the face of all the peer pressure to do otherwise. They usually give in, I understand, because the pressure is so great. I'm sorry to say that this wasn't the last time I gave in to it and broke a promise. But I feel sorry for the kids of today. It's a wide world of double-dog dares, and no grandmother's jelly to sweeten the pain.

# Football—That's the Ticket

I never knew I was doing anything wrong. I had a good reason for not watching the Cowboys game.

I'm a red-blooded guy with a background in sports that goes all the way back to the 1940s. As a ten-year-old kid I walked three miles with Billy Wayne Jones, an older boy, to Bobby White's house in east Cleburne to watch SMU play Notre Dame on television. I can tell you anything you want to know about SMU players of that era, players like Doak Walker, Kyle Rote, Dick McKissack, Henry Stollenwerck, Fred Benners, Bobby Folsom, and Jack Adkisson. Even trivial pursuit facts: Folsom later became mayor of Dallas, and Adkisson became the wrestler, Fritz von Erick.

When I was fourteen we got our own TV, and I watched all the games and kept up with all the scores that it was possible for a human to endure and keep on breathing. Later, I was the sports editor of the high school newspaper and wrote up all the games the Cleburne Yellow Jackets played. I covered the summer baseball leagues for the *Cleburne Times-Review*. Every Saturday afternoon during football season I set aside to listen to Kern Tipps call the Southwest Conference Game of the Week on radio.

When I was eighteen, Jim Browder, an older friend from Cleburne, called and invited me to sit with him in the pressbox at the Cotton Bowl as he covered the game between SMU and Texas A&M. Nowadays, he is with the *Dallas Cowboys Weekly*, but back then he was a sportswriter for the old *Fort Worth Press*. There I was, sitting beside some of the titans of the pressbox, in sportswriter heaven. I had tried to emulate them with all my small-town, fantasy-living, hero-worshiping heart. Even in my sleep, my little football-fevered brain manufactured cliches, which I used to embellish a compendium of statistics, weaving them audaciously into sweeping paragraphs of preposterous prose. I even brought these immortal write-ups with me to show off to these titans. They would marvel, as I envisioned it, at my prodigious talent.

It didn't happen. They ignored me, rightly so, and my deathless prose. But as it turned out, it didn't matter. I had an epiphany that day, a revelation that changed my life. As I sat there watching these players tugging and hauling one another to the ground, the thousands in the stands cheering them on, it occurred to me that there was only so much value that I was willing to invest in an enterprise that was, after all, just a game. I was a freshman in college and being introduced for the first time to the writings of Montaigne, Charles Lamb, and other new heroes. A world elsewhere presented itself to me, and I never again kept up with the ball scores. I still write about sports from time to time, though, and in 1980 came out with a sports book.

All of which is background for what happened during the game between the Cowboys and the 49ers. I had gone down to my farm in Hill County, cut a load of wood, and was coming back through Grandview when I was pulled over for speeding. The officer was young, and his lack of seniority had obviously forced him to work that Sunday. Maybe he desperately needed to write some citations, and there were no prospects on these empty streets. What was he to do? Then, when all may have seemed lost for him, here I come, racing down Main Street at thirty-five miles per hour.

Of course, he checked all the state-required items—license, insurance, tags, inspection sticker. He even measured the film on my windows and the tread depth on my tires. Then he glared at me, as if trying to understand the diseased brain that would not be interested in the Cowboys playoff game.

"What'd I do, officer?" I said finally.

"You were fairly flying down this street," he said coldly. "Forty in a thirty. We have kids crossing this street. You could run over somebody."

I looked back toward the vacant town. It was as a ghost town. The only sound was the low moaning of the wind as it swept through the desolate streets.

"I'm a fan of the Cowboys," I said suddenly. "But I was too far from home to get there in time for the game." I was preparing to launch into my long history as a fan when I saw him writing the ticket. "I was listening to it on the radio!" I said, as a desperate finale. It was useless.

I was in the wrong place at the wrong time, as the old saying goes. I should have been at home in front of the TV as I was supposed to be.

## There's a Past in My Future

A listener told me recently that she envied me for a having a hometown that had so much meaning in my life. I asked where she was from and she said, "Well, I went to L.D. Bell High School. There's really no hometown there, not like the one you had."

Well, of course, there must be, and wherever it is, a lot of people are proud to be associated with it. But what she meant was that she wished she had grown up in a small town and driven around a courthouse, one filled with documents that record a history of births, marriages and divorces, murders, and a million other statistics that all tell stories of their own.

She said she envied my Main Street, with hangouts like Doc McDearmons' shoe shop and Buddy Lightfoot's Café. She missed out on all the after-date, late-night gatherings at The Stadium Drive-In where we drank coffee and ate lots of unimaginably delicious hamburgers. She wished she could have gone to Shifter's Root Beer Stand on West Henderson and up to Rosedale Street in Fort Worth late at night, to Little John's, where there was the best barbecue ever served up on light bread.

She said she had had no state park like ours to go to at night, where we had sipped Salty Dogs and the boys slow-danced with future Miss Texas and Miss America and Miss Universe beauties with the waves lapping gently at the boat docks and cedar trees swaying in the soft summer breeze and a full moon reflecting off the center of the lake like the golden joy of our small-town Texas youth.

Well, I think that's what she said. It was something to that effect.

Certainly, I like my hometown and still go back there a lot. I would even like to move back there when I retire. But before you quote Thomas Wolfe to me, I'm not so sappy with sentiment that I think you can really ever go back home again. My high school building still stands, but as a branch of Hill County Junior College. The courthouse is still there, of course, but you can't drive around it anymore. Cleburne has one-way streets now. Doc has been dead for years, and there's a parking lot where his shoe shop used to be. The Stadium Drive-In is a Goodwill now. There's an H-E-B grocery where Shifter's used to be. You can't get a cup of coffee at Buddy Lightfoot's any more—it's an eye clinic now. The full moon still reflects off the Cleburne State Park lake each month but with the soft golden joy of somebody else's youth.

Why would I want to go back to a town that has changed this much? Well, even though some of my old friends have died or moved away, others are still there. And though the old hangouts are gone, we have a shared memory of them, and that's important. Those of us who issue from Southern roots seem not to be embarrassed to say that we are always trying to get back to them, one way or another. It is a characteristic of the human race, this uncontrollable urge always toward some new happiness. Schopenhauer calls it enslavement to will. Maybe the human race has never recovered from being kicked out of the Garden of Eden. We're still trying to get back to Eden.

Getting back to your hometown can soothe these mythical aches as you age. Cleburne is no Garden of Eden and I was never kicked out of it, though I did sample my share of forbidden fruit there.

I used to sit with my grandfather under his gigantic pecan tree and listen to his stories about what the town was like in his day. He was a railroad man, as I was, but the Santa Fe picked up and left Cleburne five years ago. My children were lucky enough to have heard the shop whistle blow at eight, noon, and four and to go to sleep at night hearing, as I did, the ghostly sound of freight cars bumping together in the train yard.

They heard lots of my grandfather's stories, too. Now, I have grandchildren and some stories of my own to tell.

What the listener said was ironically true. Her hometown is nowhere. Mine, too. They exist only in our memories, and our stories about them are always ever so much better than the real thing ever was.

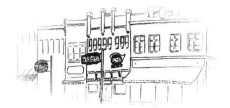

# 1995

*I wished they could be children forever, or at least spared the desperation of adolescence—the galloping hormones, cigarettes, alcohol, drugs, and the terrible burden of conformity.*

## I Left My Parts in Oklahoma

Midlothian is a better place since regular auto-repair service shops came in and put most of the shade-tree mechanics out of business. Used to be, when your transmission went out, either you got one from a wrecking yard and replaced it yourself or got a good old boy to do it in his front yard.

It's all different now. When my transmission went out, I just towed my truck up to the neatly dressed "technicians" at the new transmission repair shop and put it into their friendly hands.

Next day, prompt as you please, my friendly service manager called. "Good news and bad news," he said. "Bad news is that your transmission is messed up. Good news is that we can fix it."

The cost for this expertise: $1,700—including the clutch.

Now I know you're thinking that's a lot of money for these repairs. But what you don't know is how friendly he was and how concerned that my truck get back on the road. Friendliness is important to us small-town folk. And we like it when service managers are genuinely concerned about us.

But I guess we don't like it $1,700 worth.

"This truck is ten years old," I say. "I would feel stupid shifting the gears on a transmission that's worth more than the truck."

So you might think my friendly service manager would not be so friendly anymore after this, that he would try to accommodate someone else who would be more appreciative. But he called back later. He had more good news, much better than the old good news. He had found some parts in, uh, Oklahoma, and these were just as good as these previous, more expensive parts. With these Oklahoma parts, which he could get for a "substantial savings," he could put me back on the road for, say, $1,200.

Now, you see, a few years ago, back in the old shade-tree era, I would have been stuck with the old price. Those old mechanics, who didn't use terms like "substantial savings," would never call you back a few minutes later with a new price. They didn't have access to these parts in Oklahoma. It was the dickens back then.

Well, I was already overcome with all this friendliness and personal concern, but you'll never guess what he said when I told him that I had the silly figure of $800 in my head and couldn't seem to shake it. He said that his company would finance my transmission repair! This is something unheard of in this small town. We're familiar with financing your car and your house, but I personally have never heard of anyone financing a transmission. "My coffee-drinking buddies down at Dee-Tee's would make fun of me," I told him, "if I financed my transmission." I asked him whether he might be willing to make another call to Oklahoma instead.

Pretty soon, he called back. "I've talked to the boss," he said, "and he's willing to buy your truck from you—to help you out."

I said I was about to puddle up over all this generosity.

"Hey, we're here for you," he said.

I thought this was nice. In the old days, the shade-tree mechanic would never think to help you out like this. He usually had a yardful of old trucks already and didn't need another one. But I told him no, and wondered whether he knew of any more states he could call since Oklahoma seemed to be coming up dry lately.

Ungrateful as it sounds, I said I would just have to take my truck back and hope that Oklahoma comes through sometime this year. If he would please load up my worn-out parts and put them in the bed of the truck, I would pull it home.

I could tell that he was awfully embarrassed by my ungrateful attitude. He said that wouldn't be in my best interests because the labor charges had already reached $265. I would have to pay that, and my truck still wouldn't be fixed.

It has been a long time since anybody has been this concerned with my best interests. Let me tell you, it makes you want to sob. How could I say no to that? So I thought it over and decided I would just buy a rebuilt transmission and forget about Oklahoma.

"Even if you could find one, which you can't," he told me, looking as sad as a Christian martyr, "it would cost you more than $800. We would install it for $200, but we couldn't guarantee it."

Lucky me. I found one on the first telephone call—for $295. I brought it in, and he said installation costs, including clutch, would be $607. Again, I was unable to show my gratitude. I said I would appreciate a list of all charges, in case I had to check them out with the Better Business Bureau.

When I picked up the truck, he said he had made a mistake in his math. The total was actually $507.

After all I had put this man through, you wouldn't think he would still be interested in my well-being to the point of rechecking his math and saving me a hundred bucks.

It's such a comfort knowing that changes like this cannot help but bring big-city concerns to our small town.

· · · 🍎 · · ·

# Small Town Values

The headline of the March 3 edition of the *Waxahachie Daily Light* carried a headline saying that a local woman would begin a twenty-one-month term. Accompanying the story was a photo of an attractive woman smiling as if she had just won the lottery or been appointed to some office. I thought the twenty-one-month term did, in fact, refer to a political office.

In a sidebar, State Representative Jim Pitts is quoted as saying that this woman "is a fine, respected member of the community who made some wrong decisions." Okay, I'm thinking, she's in an opposing party, and although he disagrees with her politically he can still respect her as a community leader and pillar of small town values.

But she wasn't appointed to an office. No, she had pleaded guilty to stealing $301,888 from the First Interstate Bank of Waxahachie.

Well, not *stealing*.

As the bank manager, she was "fraudulently transferring" the money "into her own personal checking account," the news story says.

So you see, her "term" refers to her prison term.

Well, not exactly *prison*.

On March 27, she relocated to the minimum security facility at Carswell Air Force Base in Fort Worth to begin her punishment—uh, "term"—for stealing the money—I mean "transferring the funds." Actually, there's not much punishment involved. She was fined only fifty bucks along with her relocation to the military base by federal judge Jerry Buchmeyer, who also recommended that she get time off for her son's wedding. His honor could have fined her a million dollars and ordered her to repay the "transferred funds" but didn't because of her "inability to pay," the paper quoted him as saying.

In letters to the editor, some Ellis County residents expressed puzzlement by this demonstration of judicial benevolence. One writer figured that if she had stolen this much money she would have gone to prison for a very long time, with no time off for a wedding.

I visited with Representative Pitts about his helpfulness to her in this matter. One question I had was how he reconciled his support of her with his "get tough on crime platform" in last year's campaign. Another was whether taxpayers were paying for this incident three times—his salaries as public defender and congressman, and for the FDIC insurance to cover the stolen money—uh, "transferred funds."

Hoping to look like "a fine, respected member of the community" myself, I wore my best suit, boots, and flat-brimmed Stetson. I didn't have a lapel flag so I wore my Woodmen of the World Fifty-Year Pin.

Mr. Pitts is a pleasant, slender man who resembles a blond Michael J. Fox. He wore stiffly laundered Dockers, open-necked shirt, and tiny, curious loafers with little plastic cleats on the soles. His office is decorated with fine civic taste.

After my usual display of clumsy finesse, I asked my first question.

Yes, he's tough on crime, he tells me—in fact, he says he won't even defend "criminals." This woman is not a criminal, so there was no defense necessary. He merely "walked her through it," he said.

"If I ever get into trouble, will you walk me through it?" I ask.

He smiled cherubically. He said he knew that a lot of people think she just got her "wrists slapped." But twenty-one months for this offence was actually near the maximum sentence—which is twenty-four months.

"And the $301,888 she stole—uh, funds she transferred?"

"She spent it," he said. "She bought clothes at Neiman-Marcus. Cars for the kids, you know, spent it. Just keeping up with the Joneses."

Three days before this status-seeker was to begin her term at Carswell, the *Daily Light* ran one of its usual "get tough on crime" editorials. In his conclusion the editorialist wrote, "If we passed a law saying that anyone convicted of a felony gets beheaded, I can guarantee the crime rate would go down."

I didn't even flinch. I knew he didn't mean decapitation for "respected members of the community" who were only "transferring funds." He meant the nonprominent wrongdoers only—those without friends in high places.

So, the system works—if you have someone to walk you through it.

## Old Is as Old Does

Some of my baby boomer friends have turned fifty and seem to be adjusting to it with relative ease despite a youth-oriented television culture that has conditioned us to believe this is old. When I reached this milestone, I remember thinking that there were no ceremonies in our culture to ease the passage into old age as there are with birth, graduation, marriage, even death.

Except for the inevitable greetings from AARP, there is little else to signal the turn from middle to old age. Poets of earlier cultures told beautiful stories, myths that became rituals to ease the way.

Our equivalents of these poets are television writers, mainly advertising writers. They are young. They know the pre-boomer crowd doesn't buy needless items, so we are not advertiser-friendly. Try to think of a single TV commercial that doesn't denigrate longevity. Since John Wayne died, aging film characters are routinely shown whining about their lost youth. Except for Sean Connery in *The Untouchables*, Richard Farnsworth in *The Grey Fox*, and Burt Lancaster in *Atlantic City*, you would have to go all the way back to *The Treasure of the Sierra Madre* to find a dignified character over fifty other than the Duke. Films like *Cocoon* and *Dad* trivialize aging by showing these characters seeking desperately to emulate youthful folly.

Consider ads and commercials. Youth frolic on the beach and cruise in convertibles. When a gent over fifty shows up in a commercial, he sells Preparation-H, Denture Crème, or a four-door sedan that he uses to drive only to the doctor's office or the bank to admire his certificates of deposit. Women over fifty are shown in a hair-coloring, wrinkle-erasing, breast-elevating frenzy.

These are our aging myths.

Recently, I visited a friend who had retired from teaching in a small West Texas town. He now lives in a geriatric enclave in Florida. There, I learned firsthand how many people have obeyed the television and settled into a life prescribed by the AARP. He lives in this little Eden, this demi-paradise, protected from the horrors of skateboards, rock and roll, loud mufflers, and barking dogs—in fact, there is no sound there at all. It is as silent as the moon's surface. Gliding along in their gum-soled boat shoes, these specters tread so softly that they leave no footprints. Their new generic cars are also noiseless as they transport these apparitions to church, to the doctor, and to Wal-Mart, their favorite theme park. One phantom, probably about my own age, showed me all the attributes of his new car—the highlight being that it could not be dented. He demonstrated this phenomenon by pressing his thumb into the fender and beaming proudly as it popped back out like magic. "A rubber car is something to see," I said.

These artifacts live lives of perfection, with no extremes of any kind to upset them. Even the weather hardly changes. There is no crime, mainly because they own nothing a self-respecting thief would want. Who wants a top-loader VCR, a fishing lure collection, and a rubber car with a set of Walter Hagen golf clubs in the trunk?

I almost puddled to see my old friend living in this bubble of contentment. Two years ago, he rode his bike forty miles a day over the blue highways of Motley County, hiked through the rugged wilderness with his students, and swam year round in the frigid waters of Roaring Springs. I came back home after but a few days. It was just too sad. "You'd better get on back inside," I told him as I was leaving. "The temperature might drop below seventy and give you a chill." I'm overstating—he still does his vigorous exercise; he just does it in the wrong state.

And he does it in the land of the body-snatchers!

As soon as I got back home, I went out and started up my pickup and revved up its 351 Cleveland engine. The dual pipes roared like thunder. It was the rattling sound of living close to the bone when your heart is hammering and your blood is firing like premium gas, and you're wild to roar down the straightaways and around the hairpin curves of life like a seventy-year-old Paul Newman at Daytona.

・・・ 🐝 ・・・

# How Small Was My Classroom

The school ground had changed. Some of the old oak trees have been cut down to make room for parking lots and portable classrooms. The footbridge over Buffalo Creek that I crossed to get to school is blocked off now and padlocked. There is a large air-conditioner compressor located where I used to sit sometimes and eat my sack lunch. The building has new doors and storm windows. The principal's office has moved across the hall. It's a nurse's station now.

There are other changes, but the building is still there and looks the same—actually better, considering the colorful murals in the main foyer and the many other decorations put there by the teachers. So, I wasn't disappointed by the few changes in my old school.

After all, it *has* been fifty years.

On the day after Labor Day I went back to Santa Fe Elementary in Cleburne where I started on September 4, 1945. I was completing a circle that began in that three-storey, red-brick building, a circle that included twenty-two years of education and another twenty-nine years of teaching.

Principal Julie Latshaw gave me a tour. She even took my photograph sitting in my third-grade classroom. I remember the rooms I was in, all my teachers' names, and the things they taught me. Why shouldn't I? They hugged me and told me how smart I was. I peered into the room where I went to first grade. I may have heard the ghostly sound of Miss Lula Dowse's gentle instructions to open our readers and see what Dick and Jane were doing today. I looked around and saw a new generation of teachers hugging children and telling them they are smart. But I knew their future. I wished they could be children forever, or at least spared the desperation of adolesence—the galloping hormones, cigarettes, alcohol, drugs, and the terrible burden of conformity.

Everywhere, I hear that the schools need improvement. But in many ways they are better than ever. I saw a child coming down a ramp in her wheelchair. In my day, she would have been relegated to a state school for the handicapped. The lunch program insures that no child go hungry or sit outside and eat leftovers from home. Children of all races sit happily together in class and frolic together on the playground.

Though I idealize my teachers, I know that these are as good. The children, too, except for new problems such as attention deficit disorder and fetal alcohol syndrome—neither caused by schools. Other problems originate with parents, the things they value or place store by. Parents need to ask themselves whether they really do, in fact, want a good education for their children —really want them to compete with Japanese children in math, reading, physics, and the rest—or whether they want them to be athletes and cheerleaders. Do parents want their children to know about the Battle of Troy or Troy Aikman, logarithms or rap rhythms, the Pacific Ocean or "Ocean Pacific?"

The truth is not comforting: It is that youth always adopt society's values. Whatever society rewards, that's what young people strive for.

But for a single morning, I saw children learning and laughing, much the same as my generation did in that building so many years ago. How will they turn out?

I don't know. But I do know this: It is all up to us.

. . . 🐛 . . .

# Another Gift of the Magi

My brother came up from his home in Angleton to teach me how to kill deer. Jack Mann and I didn't grow up together, so he was just now getting around to this important lesson. "Get in your deer-hunting mode and let's bag one for Christmas," he said. I had no experience with such a mode. When I go to my Hill County briar patch, I generally have a walking-and-contemplating mode, a fence-repairing mode, or a wood-cutting mode. Regarding the deer population there, I have only a watching mode. As long as there are food stores and I have money, I see no need for shooting the wildlife.

Deer slaying is a bloody business. Plus the meat is so acrid that the lye and formaldehyde hunters soak it in to disguise the taste never works for me. But I wanted to see Jack, and if Mr. and Mrs. White Tail had to die to make this possible, well, things are tough all over.

It was dark when we got to the cabin, so we built a fire in the stove and talked until past midnight. Through the uncurtained windows, I watched the moon rise over the forest like the old cyclops' eye. A choir of coyotes erupted, filling the forest with their song. It ceased after a minute as abruptly as it began. Jack saw it as a kind of primordial board meeting. "Whatever it was," he said, "they got it settled."

I was a first-time deer hunter, but I was determined to go all out. At daybreak I expected to be out there in the ambuscade position, locked and loaded. But daylight came and Jack showed no sign of unzipping his sleeping bag. At eight he got up, smoked a cigarette, drank a pot of coffee, and cussed the politicians. Ten o'clock came, and he was condemning Europe. The deer were apparently lazing about the forest. Finally, I said, "Shouldn't we be out there, stalking? I think the deer are getting bored. I saw one through the window, and it appeared to be yawning."

"Hey Bud," he said, "you have to do this thing right. You don't want to get in too big a rush."

That's when I figured it out. Hunting is a primordial ritual, like the coyote serenade. It is as sacred as the Dionysian Mysteries or the Lion's Club. It may be shooting and stringing up and gutting, but it's mainly planning, getting the gear together, loading the truck with beer and other necessities. Hunting is cooking breakfast on a wood stove and eating it in camouflage suits. It's boiled coffee, cussing the government, and telling fantastic tales in the silent moon-lit night. Most of all, hunting is answering the male call from deep in the DNA, to go out there where the coyotes wail, to track, stalk, kill. The women, waiting patiently back in the den, have the fire ready for the meat. They are counting on us. We are needed.

By noon, we are finally out there, stalking. We saw one of the melodious coyotes that had performed the night before. It loped slowly toward a stand of trees, paused, and looked back over its shoulder at us before disappearing into the woods. We saw three deer, but Jack allowed them to escape into the thicket. Instead of shooting, he showed me how to follow their trail down the sandy road until they jumped the neighbor's fence.

With no father still around to impress, only a bookish, foundling brother who had rather gaze at the wildlife than shoot it, Jack never came close to pulling the trigger. It was almost as if there was an unspoken pact between us: He wouldn't kill a deer if I wouldn't recite some anti-hunting passage from *Walden*. We were just ourselves, brothers who had found each other late in life, with no sibling rivalry and no image to uphold. He passed up a chance to kill a deer, and I learned to be more tolerant of hunters.

And Mr. and Mrs. White Tail? I guess they had a Merry Christmas, too.

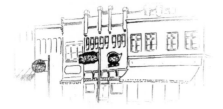

# 1996

*Wherefore this rush to portable long distance when we have never met our neighbors, much less communicated with our own souls?*

## Robert James Waller—Man or Corporation

In *The Bridges of Madison County*, the author spans deep, wide chasms of readers' emotions. In this novel, Robert James Waller spoke in ways that perhaps only women fully understand. They bought it by the millions. Yet, he is not happy.

In photos his fine cheekbones, finical mouth, and thick silver hair denote a vaguely feminine visage. In person, this aspect is offset by his rugged western gear—jeans, boots, Stetson—yet he appears to wear makeup. In any case, his days of college dean and economics teacher in Iowa are over—he's a Texas rancher now, the owner of a huge spread near Alpine.

He is also a literary corporation, come to Austin for the Texas Book Festival.

At breakfast in the Governor's Mansion, he lingers near the peripheries of the buffet table, chatting with anyone who initiates it. He is tall and slender with the heavy look of a man who wants to smoke. Though the man may want a stogie, the corporation must mingle. He wears a blue denim jacket with "The Bridges of

Madison County" patched over the left breast. "Clint Eastwood gave it to me," he says to a fan named Brenda. This would be my wife, who immediately recognized him as a corporation. "It just came in the mail one day," he goes on. He said he wears the jacket though it makes him a little self-conscious.

Later we gathered for a photograph in the capitol rotunda. The corporation and I ended up together for the photo, actually one other writer between us. "Have you read Steinbeck's story, 'The Chrysanthemums'?" I said. He said he had not and showed no interest in the reason for such a question or the horse I rode in on. I plodded onward nevertheless. "I wrote an essay about it once, in relation to your book."

He looked at me as if I were a road apple just fallen from the truck.

"Which book?" he said, "because I've written six books."

Uh oh. Piqued diva alert!

"I'm sorry, *The Bridges of Madison County*."

"I'm always identified with that book," he said. "I've written several better ones, especially *Border Music*."

Then perhaps you should consider wearing that title on your lapel, I said. Not out loud. I didn't say this out loud. I said it in my mind. I might possibly say this to the corporation but not to the man. I liked the man but wasn't sure which one I was talking to.

The photographer took a lot of shots, and the man who was a corporation said he was tired. "This is ridiculous!" were his exact words. I was sure this was the man talking, not the corporation. It was just that the man wanted to smoke again.

I saw him later when he strode through the tent where those of us who will never be corporations were autographing books that were not on the New York *Times* Best Seller list. At least forty women, looking very focused, followed in lock-step behind him. He seemed oblivious to them. This was an interesting and pleasurable sight, except that several women who were holding my book, their money in hand, dropped the masterpiece and got in step with the brigade. Other writers up and down the way who have not become corporations were similarly abandoned.

We ran into him one final time as he walked, alone this time, back toward the Governor's Mansion, where Brenda suspects he was staying. I told him it was nice of him to come. "I wasn't going to," he said. "At first I threw the invitation in the trash, but the governor's wife leaned on me."

Laura Bush is the prime mover behind this annual event.

He cupped his cigarette in his hand, shielding it from the wind, the way cowboys do. I asked what it's like for him. "Terrible!" he said. Reporters camped out in his yard. Everybody wanting this and wanting that. So he bought the ranch and hired guards and a staff just to handle his mail. Women only, he said. They're more dependable and give less trouble.

I asked about public appearances. Does he ever speak at colleges?

"No," he said. "They seem to think that if you sell too many books there must be something wrong with you. That's all right. I don't bother them and they don't bother me."

It isn't enough that millions of readers love him enough to keep *The Bridges of Madison County* on the *Times* Best Seller list for 165 weeks and make him into a corporation. Robert James Waller the man wants to be accepted by the literati.

I have heard that writers who have earned the respect of the literati but who haven't been on the *Times* Best Seller list for even one week have demeaned *The Bridges of Madison County*. I have heard publishers who have never had a *Times* best seller demean it. I have heard writers who have never had a book published demean it. Even Waller himself diminished it by saying he had written better books and was tired of being associated with it alone.

Who is ever happy?

Consider the wisdom of Shakespeare, a writer who managed to avoid literary incorporation, during his lifetime, anyway:

*O God! Methinks it were a happy life,*
*To be no better than a homely swain;*
*To sit upon a hill, as I do now,*
*To carve out dials quaintly, point by point,*
*Thereby to see the minutes how they run,*
*How many make the hour full complete;*
*How many hours bring about the day;*
*How many days will finish up the year;*
*How many years a mortal man may live.*

• • • ❧ • • •

# Don't Be a Fool, Stay in School

The newspaper carried a story the other day with the headline, "Click ties crime to social ills." The implication is that the Dallas police chief has come up with a revolutionary idea, that poor and uneducated people go to prison a lot. This idea is as old as the beginnings of civilization. The ninth and tenth commandments are property laws. Property laws appear even earlier in Hammurabi's Code. Those who owned the property, as today, made the laws.

The first American to link crime to social conditions was John P. Altgeld in his book of 1890, *Our Penal Machinery and its Victims*. Clarence Darrow, the great defense lawyer, updated these ideas in his own book *Crime, Its Causes and Treatment*, in 1922.

Michael Parenti, a modern social scientist, has further updated them. In his book *Democracy for the Few*, he offers a good deal of evidence that crime goes down as employment goes up.

These authors do not suggest that all poor and uneducated people break the laws and that the educated and rich are always law-abiding. A few educated executives can steal more money in a single holdup, as in the savings and loan thefts of the 1980s, than a thousand muggers could steal in a thousand lifetimes. In one white-collar stickup in Dallas, two land developers stole over a hundred million dollars from the Empire Savings and Loan. Such holdups occurred all over the country during the last decade. Our grandchildren, it is said, will have to pay for these big heists.

What they do suggest is that most property lawbreakers are made desperate by social conditions. They are usually punished to the limit of the law. As Chief Ben Click points out, seventy to eighty percent of prison inmates are illiterate, addicted to drugs, or come from abusive homes. While the overall unemployment rate may be five percent, he goes on, it is sixty percent in their neighborhoods. These lawbreakers have no money, status, or self-esteem. They have no access to F. Lee Bailey for their defense and end up with long jail terms—plea bargained by public defenders. While in prison they are tutored by more experienced wrongdoers and use their time there to perfect their skills in crime.

For stealing a hundred million dollars, the two Dallas crooks got seven to twenty years. A few years ago in Houston, a lower-level three-time offender named Odis Chappell got thirty-five years for stealing a can of Spam. The writer Molly Ivins has studied these matters for years and has written that, since it costs over $14,000 per year to imprison someone, it would have been cheaper just to buy Odis a lifetime supply of Spam.

Odis and his colleagues wouldn't take up this line of work if other, more respectable employment, such as that of politician or banker, were available to them. Petty thievery is a low-status job and dangerous, often requiring that these burglars navigate about in the night with a flashlight. These activities are unattractive to educated people.

Chief Click believes that the uneducated poor are adrift in a river, and we must "walk back up the river and figure out why they're falling in." We already know this. Algeld and Darrow explained it many years ago. Parenti is explaining it today. It is just that not very many people are listening.

· · · ❦ · · ·

## Washing and Irony

When Marilyn and husband Jim had reached that longed-for point in their married lives when their children were grown, his dental practice flourishing, finances in good shape, they could finally look forward to an easier life. They would enjoy the grand-children, travel, take up hobbies—in short, harvest the fruit of their hard work and sacrifice.

Then, like the thief that breaks in and robs you of all your valu-ables, disaster struck.

One of life's cruelest ironies is that Alzheimer's disease often hits the most able-bodied while the ones with dilapidated bodies, like Marilyn's father, live out their final, painful days with perfect brains. Her mother, in good physical health, began wearing her slip outside her dress, going without bathing, hiding all her pos-sessions, letting some of her bills go unpaid and paying others several times. She also began telling everyone she was pregnant.

Like millions of others today who find themselves faced with this situation, Marilyn became the parent of her mother and father.

Unfortunately, the money-vultures had swooped down and devoured much of her parents' savings. She signed them up for Home Health and Meals on Wheels. She got them hospital beds and put them in the den. She took over their finances. She cooked, cleaned, gave them their medication, dressed and bathed them.

The first time she bathed her father, he cried. They had never been close before; she had always viewed him as uncaring, cruelly distant. When she disrobed him and washed him tenderly, he said, "I want you to know that I would have done this for you."

From that moment, all was forgiven, she said.

There had been a family secret between them. It was now washed away. There had been a young housekeeper. They would go riding in the car, the three of them, when Marilyn was but a child. There were irrepressible memories of walking down the road while he stayed in the car with the housekeeper. Then, agitation in the household, and the housekeeper was gone.

Marilyn had eventually told her mother.

Of course, her mother already knew about the car rides, the pregnancy, the regular checks that went out for the child's upkeep. "I wouldn't be surprised if a brother or a sister shows up on my doorstep someday," Marilyn said.

Her parents spent their last days together in the twin hospital beds, he flicking the television remote, she prattling on endlessly about being pregnant. "And I want you to know," she told him pointedly and ceaselessly, "that this baby isn't yours!"

Marilyn smiles now about her mother's final act of one-upmanship and is content with the way it all worked out. It was hard, she said, but the closeness she found with her father deepened her understanding of the healing powers of selflessness.

Soon, she and her husband Jim leave for mission work in the impoverished towns along the Mexico-Texas border. He to give free dental care to the people there and she to donate to the needs of the heart and spirit, a currency she accumulated at her parents' bedside.

Being parents to our mothers and fathers is hard. But it is humbling, and it fills the spiritual purse.

• • • ❦ • • •

# Whiners Never Die, They Just Grumble Away

If I don't whine, it's because I was brought up by my grandmother, who never got around to knowing what a stoic was because she was too busy being one. In 1918 she and my grandfather lived on a squalid farm near Egan, in Johnson County. That year, she lost her baby to measles, her twin brother to bomb fragments in France, and a cotton crop due to my grandfather's typhoid fever. He was bedridden, and neighbors helped get some of the crop in. She had a three-year-old and my mother, a newborn, to care for. Groceries were a luxury, and she had to carry water from a neighbor's well.

By the time the Depression came, my grandparents were affected less than others. When you hit bottom at the age of twenty-three, things can't get any worse.

When she told me these stories, she said she was lucky compared to Job, the Bible character who never whined though he lost his farm and seven children and had to put up with boils and a nagging wife.

Television, today's substitute for Bible stories, promotes whining. It makes money by exploiting dissatisfaction—on talk shows and in interviews with celebrities and politicians all the way up to the White House. Whiners always have more than they need already but whine for what they don't have and because others, who don't deserve it, might get too much, too. Celebrities whine about their image, about tabloids, and the high cost of divorce. Televangelists whine about liberals and the high cost of raising money. Right-wing talk show hosts with seeming unlimited airtime whine about the biased media. Athletes making millions whine that some other running back or outfielder or basketball shooter gets a bigger contract.

Men whine about President Clinton's lack of ethics but are really whining because he's better looking than they are, smarter, and has all the girlfriends he wants. Women spend billions each year on cosmetics, diet books, and sexy clothes, then whine about sexual harassment if someone they aren't attracted to tells them how great they look.

All this whining starts at birth. Babies, of course, howl a lot at a very high decibel level. At a certain age, they switch to that wretched whiny caterwauling that we are all familiar with: "He won't let me do that." "I don't ever get to be first." "Why do I always have to clean up my room?" It never occurs to them that they are lucky to have a room. Animals whine, too, especially those that stay around humans. Maybe whining is inborn, but so is "going to the bathroom," which is customarily tended to in private.

A few days before my sister Helen died of cancer, I said to her, "I know people who whine if their wrist is sore from typing and have to park in handicapped parking spaces. Nobody would blame you if you complained. Why don't you?"

"Hon," she said, "I would if I thought it would do any good."

A man I knew who was handicapped spent his life stoically taking care of his big fat wife, who stayed in bed and whined about her imagined ailments. When he died, she lost weight and started going dancing on Saturday nights.

Maybe what Helen meant was that whining may be good for you and make you live longer, but it's wrong. And, besides, who's going to be around to listen to the whiners when the rest of us are all dead?

· · · ❦ · · ·

# Just Call 1-800 Walden

Improving technology has always made it easier for people to stay in touch with one another—but is the communication equal to the technology? If you can think of little or nothing to say to your neighbors or townspeople when you meet them face to face at the bank or grocery store, then how is a cellular phone going to help you? Lots of people talk on their phones while driving on the freeway. Smoking in the car and in restaurants used to be a national pastime; but now it's talking on the phone. Soon, I suspect, when you go out to eat, you will be asked, "Cell phones or non?" The other day I saw two people in the cafeteria line talking on cell phones. Were they talking to each other? "The eggplant looks good today," I imagined one saying to the other.

Voice mail. E-mail. Fax. Cell phone. Beeper. They have become necessities. I think communication is the least important function of the latter two. For fidgety people, cell phones replace cigarettes. For status-seekers, they are objects of conspicuous consumption, as pagers are, and provide the appearance of importance. Men wear their phones high on their belts, as Shane wore his gun. Some, I am given to understand, have acquired a good deal of speed with them too.

This need for relentless communication puzzles me. Okay, business is probably enhanced. More money. I get it. But these freeway babblers are in such a hurry! They rush down the free-ways and streets, exceeding the speed limit, cutting each other off, running stop lights—why? Is it to close some international business deal? Or are they heeding some cell phone call urging them to get to Wal-Mart and pick up the cat food before the blue light special goes off?

A lot of people I know still operate in the old-fashioned way—home phones, phone booths, and posted mail. I still write a lot of letters—and others do, too. I know because I receive a lot of them. Most people prefer e-mail, and I like it, too, except that it can't be tied with a ribbon and laid in a Pangburn's candy box and stored in a trunk at the foot of the bed. The thirty-five letters from my Uncle Dock, handwritten on YMCA stationary during the final seven months of his life in World War I, would not be the same on e-mail.

I am not opposed to progress. At one time, smoke signals and tom-toms were high-tech and thought to be vulgar by tribal cranks, who preferred messenger runners. Henry David Thoreau, the ultimate tribal crank, complained of the post office, saying that he never received over two or three letters that were worth the postage. While admitting that the telegraph would give Maine an opportunity to talk with Texas, he wondered whether Maine and Texas had anything of value to say to one another.

Those addicted to cell phones seem genuinely fascinated with them and enjoy them as if they were toys. Yet, these addicts seem simply to be lonely. Before cell phones came along, and before air conditioning, radio, and television brought everyone indoors, neighbors combated loneliness and boredom by gossiping together on wide front porches. They dropped in on one another unannounced and played dominoes or talked the evenings away. Again, to be fair, loneliness and boredom are not recent problems. Those who depend on gadgets or other people for stimulation have always been most susceptible. Thoreau observed that, despite the fact that earth is a part of the Milky Way, people of his day were lonely, too. "After a night's sleep," he writes in *Walden*, "everyone says, 'tell me anything new that has happened to a man anywhere on the globe.' And he reads over his breakfast rolls that a man has had his eyes gouged out...never dreaming the while that...he has but a rudiment of an eye himself."

Wherefore this rush to portable long distance when we have never met our neighbors, much less communicated with our own souls? Why be hastened by the urgent call of technology? Again, to paraphrase Thoreau: If the engine whistles, let it whistle until it is hoarse. If the bell rings, why should we run? The summons usually isn't worth the run.

What, then, would be a message worth the sending and worthy of receiving? Thoreau writes of a prince who once sent the following message by courier: "I wish to diminish the number of my faults but cannot come to the end of them."

What a message! What a message!

# Old Dog Walking

Lindon had noticed Fred's occasional clumsiness, especially in the mornings. Fred would sometimes stumble as his front legs suddenly gave way. Lindon passed it off as a typical characteristic of old age. Fred is twelve. At other times, he seemed all right, trotting along as usual behind Lindon's wheelchair.

Comes then Lindon's agitated voice on the telephone: "Dad, you'd better get over here and help me with Fred. He can't walk!"

Lindon was even more agitated when I got there. Fred was on the floor. When he saw me, he tried to get up but couldn't. He struggled to his feet momentarily, then swayed crazily like a drunkard and fell over on his face.

After the veterinarian examined him, Fred came out teetering behind Lindon's wheelchair. Fred had bone spurs on his spine, the veterinarian said, pinching the nerves. He was becoming paralyzed. "I can refer you to a specialist," he said. "Surgery can run $1,500, and he might not even make it through it. Even if it's successful, you still have an old dog."

Then, he said the unthinkable. "You may have to consider putting him to sleep."

To Lindon, this would be a gross betrayal of Fred. When he can't walk anymore, kill him. "I'm taking him home," Lindon said. "I can take care of him."

Before we got out the door, Fred fell over on his face again and couldn't get up. "You can't take him home, Lindon!" I said "He's in too bad a shape!"

Ordinarily, it's not a good idea to tell your thirty-five-year-old son what he can't do. But sometimes dads can't help being dads. "Look," I went on, "they can keep him here and give him his medication. You can pick him up when he's better."

Lindon called the clinic every day. "He's not getting any better," he told me. "They've given up on him. I want you to go with me and help me bring him home."

With all the pain and sadness in the world, what happens to an old dog is trivial in comparison. But all of us felt a deep sense of helplessness over it, its cruel irony. Fred, an Airedale-spaniel mixture, heavy on the Airedale, has been Lindon's constant friend and companion since a year after his accident. Human friends may go south but Fred is as constant as the Dog Star.

We all wanted to do something—but what? I went over and gave Fred a bath. Lindon's mother and sister went and bought a wagon for Lindon to pull him around in. His brother suggested a set of wheels for his front end, as he seemed to be able to use his back legs a bit. What bothered us most was: what about Fred's bowels and bladder needs? We would have to build him a rack, the veterinarian said, so he wouldn't be lying in it. None of us had any idea how to do that.

The next morning Lindon called and said he had been up all night helping Fred. We all shook our heads. How could this go on? Just taking care of himself is a big job for Lindon. How could he take care of a paralyzed dog?

After Lindon was injured in 1982, I spoke with a doctor in Oregon about DMSO, a solvent said to relieve inflammation and which was being used experimentally for paralysis. I asked the vet for a bottle of it. "Can't hurt," he said.

Lindon applied it with the faith of a Bible martyr. A day later, he called. "Guess who's walking?" The joy in his voice told me the answer.

I rushed over, and there was Fred, up on all fours, wobbly, like a newborn deer, but walking. Was Fred healed by dimethyl sulfoxide's holy unction?

Veterinarians are convinced that it can't be the DMSO. Yet, he continues to improve. A great pervading pall of sadness has been lifted. We don't know how or why, but we know it's a welcome sight—a devoted old dog, trotting along behind his master's wheelchair again.

· · · 🐞 · · ·

# C.W. Moss, Driver of Hard Bargains

My regular plumber was all backed up, and I needed a leaking valve replaced under the lavatory. Since I already had the new valve, the plumber could make fifty bucks in five minutes, and my wife could brush her teeth with cold water for a change. So, I had a bright idea. Life is short. There's a big wide world out there. Live a little, I told myself.

I called an UNKNOWN PLUMBER.

Just picked him out of the Yellow Pages. Out he came in no time flat. I looked him over. He had on a starched shirt and trousers and carried a big satchel. He was a pleasant-looking guy with a big smile. Very un-plumberly. He looked like C.W. Moss, the kid in *Bonnie and Clyde* who drove the getaway car. This was an astounding contrast with my regular plumber, who smokes Camels, has hairy shoulders, and wears low-riding pants that expose a wide section of his rear geography when he goes under the sink. "You're the plumber?" I say.

"Yessir," says C.W., his little fat cheeks shining like ceramic.

I look out front. There's a new red van sitting there. "Where's your pickup?" say I. "The one with the PVC pipes hanging over the side and the moldy commodes stacked in the bed."

I was suspicious. Things are not looking good. In any case, I show him the bathroom. See it through, I say. I show him the new valve I bought.

"You'll like ours a lot better," he says. "It'll work a lot better for you."

"How much for the whole job?" say I.

At this point, I learned the role of the satchel.

He opens it and extracts a big book, the pages encased in plastic. He thumbs through it, stops on a page, and moves his little antiseptic finger down a line of figures. "That'll be $104, sir," he says, smiling. "Plus tax."

I was aware of a sudden rapid heartbeat, and my glasses fogged over. I took them off and cleaned them on my shirttail. That's when I noticed his feet. Over his shoes, he wore hospital booties, the kind surgeons wear. If I had seen this at first, the house call would have ended at the door. I can't help it. I try to be liberal. I work at it. Things change and I must adapt. I know this. I was willing to try to take a plumber seriously who drove a new red van and looked like C.W. Moss in a starched shirt and carried a leather satchel. I tried to be understanding. It's a new world. Don't be a Luddite. Get with it. I was willing to try to do this.

But the little plastic antiseptic booties?

Nah.

I laughed, really laughed hard—at myself mainly, as I wrote out the check for the $29.95 service call. I had tried to be mature through the entire farce, but at this point I did something childish. I made the check out to "Overpriced Plumbing Corp." It was silly, but it turned out to be a good thing.

It prompted a call from the owner. He said he always tried to follow up on "negatives."

I'm glad he did because I had a question: "Are you running a successful business at these prices? The reason I asked," I said, "is that you could, theoretically, send out a plumber, who quotes an exorbitant price and when it is rejected by an old tightwad like myself, you could make $29.95 in five minutes. If the victim, I mean customer, accepts the job, you've made quite a large profit. I know you're not that kind of guy, though."

He is not, he says. He has five of these red vans, each equipped with a million dollars' worth of tools. He has a million dollars' worth of liability insurance. He pays his plumbers seventeen dollars an hour and provides heath insurance. Because of this, each service call costs him, he said, forty-six dollars.

"I'm just a guy from Oklahoma," he went on, "who came to the Midlothian area to set up a plumbing business that didn't have the usual stereotypes. Our plumbers wear the hospital shoe covers to keep from bringing germs from house to house. They're even tested for drugs."

He had a good point. I understand that there are a lot of very busy professional people today who work long hours and carry leather satchels, too, and who have more important things on their minds than comparing plumbers' fees. They might appreciate the red van, starched shirt, leather satchel, and big tally book. Single mothers, too, who probably appreciate their plumber wearing sterile shoe covers and sparing them the rear body geography.

But there's one question I didn't have the guts to ask: Do his guys get teased a lot by the old-time plumbers?

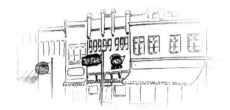

# 1997

*I know things change, but I remember
Christmases when everybody's house at
night didn't look like Caesars Palace.*

## Purple Press

It's encouraging to see that there are so many newspaper readers who are interested in thoughtful writing. The *Dallas Morning News* is a nationally respected paper, generally well written, with Pulitzer Prizes and many fine writers. But even great Homer sometimes nods. A columnist recently attributed a line to Proust that originated with Shakespeare, and she caught heck from readers about it. This same columnist used "apocryphal" to mean "spurious," or "false." I didn't write in, but the distinction is that it means "hidden" or "secret." Many people use it to mean "false" these days, so I guess the erroneous definition has become "correct." I assume the change in definition came about when important people began referring to secret religious writings, "apocrypha," as false.

I did write, however, in response to a reporter in the *Waxahachie Daily Light* (no Pulitzers, no fine writers) who wrote that six officers tried to "disburse" a group of bystanders late at night after an extended Fourth of July party. I wrote that standing on the street at any hour is free, and police have no right to disburse anyone of their hard-earned money simply for observing

Independence Day. If the police are so underpaid, I wrote, why don't they disburse the tourists who regularly congregate in downtown Waxahachie to gawk at the courthouse? They have money in those little pouches strapped about their middles. The editor ignored my letter. He probably thought I needed to be disbursed so that I would have no more money for stamps.

I wrote to the *Cleburne Times Review* (once had very good writers: Harold V. Ratliff, Jack Proctor, Jim Browder) to request more information on a news story about a man who had been hit on the head and had come out of a "comma." I wondered whether the comma he came out of was before a conjunction introducing a dependent clause, a comma separating nouns in a series; or maybe the comma he came out of was one used to set off parenthetical material. I never found out because my letter was never answered, much less printed.

But others' letters are printed, one recently to the *Morning News* deploring the thoughtless use of "inexhaustible" to describe a man who had killed himself with exhaust fumes. Later, I saw another example of deplorable diction. In the September 28 edition, the *News* reported that ValuJet was "swamped" with reservations after being allowed to resume service after one of its airliners crashed. It crashed, as everyone knows, in a Florida swamp. Just this morning, this paper said that the Russian government has taken over the alcohol industry to try to pay off "staggering debts." In an editorial, I noticed the following mixture: "The question for the fed is no longer whether to raise rates... but when it should pull the trigger on a rate cut." Is it too much to ask that the writer decide whether the fed needs to shoot something or slice it?

And this odd choice of words from a *News* story on male impotence: "... [I]f the root problem is treated, the impotence will disappear." Oh.

Cliches abound. In that same September 28 edition on the business page, I marked some of them: "position themselves as major players," "floodgates really opened," "mount last-minute effort," "breaking a long stalemate," "remained at risk," "get an edge," "break from the ranks," and "get the lion's share." One cliched metaphor was so muddled that I couldn't interpret it: "the cap on the audience reach has been upped." What on earth?

I wonder which errors readers dislike most. For me, it's padding. Consider this story, again from the *Morning News*, October 3 edition. The headline says: "Drought appears over for most of Texas, experts say." This same information is repeated five times in the seven-paragraph story. The "drought is now history." Rains "have broken the drought." "The drought is officially over." "The state seems to have emerged from several months of drought." And, finally, thankfully, "the drought is considered over."

There is certainly no drought of bad writing all around, and I hope that readers continue to flood the editors' pages with their scolding letters.

· · · 🍒 · · ·

# The Leaving of Bob

April was a cruel month for Texas writers. Their greatest friend and supporter, Bob Compton, retired. Since 1976, he has labored as books editor for the *Dallas Morning News*, deciding which books from among the hundreds he received each day would be reviewed. Such exposure is gold for an author, and Texas writers of merit had an advantage with him—as did Texas reviewers, who also owe him a major debt. In a tribute to him at the meeting of the Texas Institute of Letters last week at Houston, one such writer, Marshal Terry, said that before Compton, reviewers weren't even paid.

For a lot of writers, that reviewer's paycheck has been the only thing in their wallet other than their children's pictures. Before Chris Tucker became editor of *D Magazine*, money was scarce, he told me—and Bob Compton was the first editor to give him a paycheck. Other writers like Clay Reynolds and Joe Holley—same thing. Both began reviewing for Compton as young English teachers, then eventually saw their own books reviewed in his pages.

Some of the writers he has helped, like Rick Bass, leave Texas after making good but still keep in touch with him. They couldn't get away from him if they tried. He calls them up, several times if necessary, to make sure that they don't miss this or that literary function. "Hey, man, you did say you'd be there, didn't you? Hey, don't worry—I've got your tickets."

I got him to slow down for a private visit at the TIL meeting. We walked the lush grounds surrounding the Houstonian Hotel, then sat in a swing under a stand of live oaks. He's from a small town, and I figured that if I could get him into that old-timey swing he would tell me all about himself. He's notoriously laconic, a rare and endearing trait in this era of unlimited self-disclosure. He has other rare traits. Jim Lehrer, another writer he has aided, said that Compton always worked on Christmas Eve so that the married reporters, like himself, could be with their families. Afterwards, it wasn't unusual for him to show up and help the fathers assemble all the Santa Claus toys.

Back in his hometown of Teague, in Freestone County, he worked in his father's lumberyard. Later, he graduated from SMU and served in the Navy during World War II. His career includes but three papers, beginning in Pampa, then in Garland, finally moving to the *Morning News* in 1957, where he swapped sports for books. "Every now and then," he said, "a big sports story would come along and I would say, 'man, what I would give to write that!'"

He isn't known primarily as a writer anymore, but he's a good one. The reports he filed from the sites of special literary events would be models for journalism students because of their simple, fact-filled, compressed style. Nothing mean, cute, or trite. No silly puns. Nothing calculated to draw attention away from the story to himself. I'm probably not the only one encouraging him to write his memoirs. He is one of only three book editors the *Morning News* has ever had.

The TIL meeting was his final story as editor. At his retirement party last week his assistant, Cheryl Chapman, said he called her from Houston to verify the story; then he added that he was surprised by the tribute he received. "They said a lot of nice things about me," her told her—"but don't print that!"

She didn't—she told a roomful of reporters instead.

## Hard Hands, Soft Heart

Midlothian is a small town and therefore has only one native who has fought three world champion boxers. Donnie Fleeman is low-key about this and content that the local paper ignores him while profiling the ice cream stick sculptor, the woman who shook hands with Charles Bronson, and the fisherman who caught the biggest catfish. Maybe the local gazette would be impressed only if he had won the championship.

His fists are oaken, but his heart is too tender for such a profession. After defeating Ezzard Charles, the former heavyweight champion who had beaten Joe Louis, Fleeman said, "I didn't like knocking out a great champion, but I had to do it. It was my job."

He now lives near Red Oak, but his parents still live in the same house in Midlothian where he grew up. His father is ninety-two and, his mother is ninety. He checks on them daily. Afterward, he met me for coffee at Dee-Tee's, a good place to discuss the higher forms of boxiana.

He's tall with massive hands and fingers, but his forearms are no larger than the trunks of average-size trees. He worries that his waist may have ballooned to thirty-two or thirty-three inches. I poked him in the stomach, and it felt more or less like ordinary cast iron to me. At sixty-three, he looks trimmer than most men in their twenties. But I didn't bring this up. He is not one to make idle talk about himself. He prefers important topics—like his grandchildren. Ordinarily, this is my favorite topic too, but since he's the only man I know in Midlothian who has knocked out Ezzard Charles, I thought this would be an interesting topic as well.

The other two heavyweight champions defeated him. He fought Muhammad Ali in Miami Beach on February 21, 1961. The fight was stopped in the seventh round when the referee learned that Fleeman was fighting with a broken sternum. It was broken three weeks before in a fight with Pete Rademacher. He believes he might have beaten Ali if he could have used both arms. "Ali didn't hit very hard," he said. "But he was fast as lightning and just wore you down."

He also lost a decision to Sonny Liston, who went on to flatten just about everybody in one round until he ran into Ali in 1964.

Fleeman made a good living in boxing but nothing like boxers make today, he said. His usual paycheck per fight was around

$4,000, which he got for the Ali fight, but he limited himself to ten or twelve fights a year. Nowadays, fighters with less skill than he had fight two or three times a year for a million or more.

He got started boxing at Midlothian High School. City boys made the severe mistake of teasing him about his country ways, so he was forced to make them cry. He spent so much time in the principal's office, he said, that the principal finally told him that if he liked to fight so much, he should get some boxing gloves. Then he would be free to fight all he wanted. The next day he brought the gloves to school and every day thereafter. He said he took those gloves everywhere he went.

His first professional fight was on July 18, 1955, at Waxa-hachie, where he knocked out Billy Watson in seven rounds. He won twenty-five of his next twenty-seven fights, eighteen by knockout. When he retired after the Ali fight, his record stood at thirty-seven wins, eleven losses, and one draw. This is a good record, excellent, in fact, because he was really a light-heavy-weight fighting heavyweights.

Anyone would think that fighting Ali would be the highlight of his career, but he said he got more satisfaction out of beating Buddy Turman, the "darling" of the Dallas sportswriters. Turman was the Texas fighter they hoped would make it big. "He was just a pretty boy," Fleeman said.

And the toughest opponent he ever fought? Certainly, that would be Ali or Liston. Wrong on both counts.

"It was some old country guy in Milan, Italy," he said, "that filled in when my scheduled opponent dropped out. I can't even remember his name. Ali and Liston played patty-cake compared to him. Nobody ever hit me like that old country boy did."

For the record, the country boy's name was Sante Amonti.

As Fleeman drove away, I imagined a man in his sixties, in some remote Italian village, showing his grandchildren a yellowed newspaper clipping of the night he upset the great American boxer from the big city called Midlothian, Texas.

· · · 🦎 · · ·

# The Joy of Anagnorisis

In the beginning were the words, and the words were *interregnum, phylliform, debouchment, mostaccioli, bhalu, dasyure,* and *abecedarius.* These were but several of the words spelled correctly by Effie Fletcher and Carol Coterill on their way to being finalists in the Dallas County Senior Spelling Bee competition held recently at the Scottish Rite Hospital in Dallas. The other twenty-nine contestants, five of them men, performed mightily but dropped out one by one during the *epitasis,* a word they couldn't spell correctly. Ironically, it means the part in a play leading up to a catastrophe.

I was a judge, along with Bettye Banks and Elena Cortez. A local well-known disc jockey—I forget his name—canceled at the last minute, and I took his place. Maybe he was afraid he would have to know how to spell. He needn't have worried. We had the words before us with the correct spellings. Mary Musgrave, a librarian in DeSoto, was the pronouncer—a difficult task.

It was an interesting event with a large audience cheering on their family members. It is sponsored annually by the City of Dallas. Vicki Smith, the Public Information Officer for Senior Affairs, promised me that I would enjoy it and that I wouldn't have to listen to a speech.

I did enjoy it, especially the talents of the participants. They represented Senior Centers from all over Dallas County. They had studied for months from a list of over three thousand words.

As the contestants were reduced to these two, both from the DeSoto Center, the words became more difficult. Suspense built. On and on they went, coolly dispensing with words most of us had never heard of or even seen in print. *Byssinosis. Dugong. Vinaigrette. Bisagre. Crystosphene. Leucoryx. Aposiopesis.* Each they spelled without a bobble. We may be here until the twenty-first century, I remember thinking.

It also occurred to me how worthwhile such a program is for the community in a time when popular culture almost totally ignores the generation past the age of sixty, unless it is demeaning it. Commercial television depicts this age group as either infantile or addled, and always as an object of derision. This stereotype has developed because youthful television writers think there must be something wrong with a group that doesn't buy the ephemeral products sold on television.

Then, Ms. Coterill was given the word *anagnorisis.* It sounded like *anagnoreesis.* That is the way Ms. Coterill spelled it.

"Wrong," said the chief judge, Ms. Banks. The word was turned over to Ms. Fletcher, who asked for another pronunciation, then promptly spelled it correctly. It means, "an incident in a play in which a character discovers the true nature of his or her situation."

Ms. Fletcher then spelled *bergschrund* to win the contest—and a cash prize of $150. She and Ms. Coterill go on to the finals in Temple on September 22.

"Do you ever use any of these words?" I asked the winner.

"No," she said, "but I heard one of them on TV once and knew what it meant."

"You heard one of these words on TV?"

"Sure. On *Chicago Hope,* someone said to get the spignometer. I knew what it meant because it was one of our words. It's a blood pressure machine." I didn't say anything, but I was thinking that they were probably hooking this spignometer up to someone over sixty who was depicted as either infantile or addled.

This elevated my blood pressure just thinking about it.

· · · 🍂 · · ·

## I Just Don't Want the Fax, Ma'am

Dealing with the business world is a continuing source of horripilation for me. For the past ten years or so, I have noted that sales personnel know less and less about the products they sell. So, after many times of going after something like a heater coil and coming home and finding a motorcycle helmet in the box, I am now wary of all purchases.

But not wary enough. The following weirdness happened because I am a typical husband and do what typical husbands do. I waited until the day of my wife's birthday party to go shopping. But I would be getting a fax machine, which should be an easy purchase.

Not easy. The Super Wal-Mart in Cleburne had a million items I didn't need or want but not one fax machine. The only other store that had them would be Radio Shack. This store had two to choose from. I selected the least expensive one and wrote out the check. I didn't want to be late for the party so I didn't open the box before leaving the store. I trusted that the box did, in fact, contain a fax machine and not a motorcycle helmet. My wife doesn't even have a motorcycle.

It wasn't a helmet. It was actually a fax machine. But there was a message from the saleswoman on my answering machine.

She had given me the more expensive model by mistake. Would I please send a check for the extra amount?

I called her and told her that, no, I didn't want the more expensive model, that I had selected the one I wanted.

"Well, could you bring it back and exchange it?"

"That would be a sixty-mile round trip," I said. "I'm tired and my wife's party starts in an hour. I'll come in next week and do that—or you can come and get this one if you like."

I explained to Brenda what had happened, and she shrugged. She said she wanted a Sony portable phone with caller-ID anyway.

There were three calls from the saleswoman on the answering machine when we got home from the party. She would be driving to Midlothian that very night—Sunday night, in the rain—to swap out the fax machines.

At ten-thirty, I met her and her husband at the Exxon station downtown. I told her I didn't want the other machine, that she could take it on back with her. How was I to know this was, in fact, the machine she wanted me to have? "I just want it to be over," I told her.

I waited several hours the next morning for the formerly frantic saleswoman to call and thank me for cooperating with her and to tell me that that she was returning my check. Of course, no such call came that morning, or any morning thereafter. So I called the bank to stop payment on the check, which I knew would cost fifteen dollars. By this time, I was thinking I would have been better off if it had been a motorcycle helmet.

I would like to stop payment on a check, I said.

This could not be done, I was told. To stop payment on a check without coming in person, I would need a fax machine.

· · · 🐛 · · ·

# Where the Cactus Blooms

Jon McConal has covered the Texas circuit for the Fort Worth *Star-Telegram* for many years and has listened to thousands of stories in order to get material for his columns. These are tales of hardship, dedication, triumph, and dreams rent and blown asunder. He takes many pages of notes, scrawls them hurriedly in spiral notebooks. He knows how to ask the right questions and to withhold judgment. If he figures into a story, it is always in a supporting role, deep background. Centerstage are the small-town denizens and eccentrics whose inarticulate tales he transforms into his characteristic idyllic prose. He seldom allows himself the luxury of personal reminiscence.

The other day he called and said he wanted to visit his old home place near Midlothian, where he lived back in the 1940s. He wanted to see where he went to high school and to church. Of course, these buildings were long since dust, casualties of progress. There's a house where the Midlothian Church of Christ was, and J.R. Irvin Middle School stands on the spot where the old high school used to be.

He guided me down the Old Fort Worth Highway to his old home site a few miles north of town. "There's the fence we built," he said. The wire was rusted and the cedar fence posts were leaning, but it was still there. Nothing else remained but a windmill tower. We crawled under the fence and walked through the cactus and bluebonnets and stood on the concrete foundation of his old house. "My brother and I slept here, and that was our mother and daddy's bedroom over there," he said, pointing the way. Hundreds of rusty nails lay everwhere, the framing studs also gone to dust.

A few feet away were the ghostly remains of the bunkhouse where the whole family had to live for a while. He looked north, up the hill, and his tone grew wistful. He said, "My daddy was the valedictorian of his college class and a shrewd cattle and horse trader, but he didn't know anything about farming. He bought this place and we spent the first year filling in that draw to stop the erosion. He spent all the money he had, and we all worked together to get it done. Then, the first year we were here, a terrible ice storm came and wiped out everything we did. Just slid down the hill and took everything with it. Everybody laughed at him for buying this land, and he laughed about it too. But I think he nearly lost his mind over it. It like to have killed him."

He squatted down and picked up a handful of dirt the way farmers do and let it sift down to the ground. "I interview so many people who tell me there's no way I could understand what they've been through," he went on. "Believe me, I understand."

I went over by the cactus patch and left him alone with his recollections. I bent down and observed the plants up close. I never knew how beautiful they were. Their yellow blossoms are wide and encompassing, their petals like golden bowls. They come from hardiness and strength and have an inner sweetness. They survive.

# There's a Clicker in Raymond's Drawers

Anyone would know, seeing my mother's apartment, that something is wrong. Her kitchen is empty, as is the inside of her refrigerator. In her room, everything that isn't too heavy to move is hidden. A curio cabinet in the corner is bare.

When I picked her up for a dental appointment, we had to search for her purse. I went through the drawers of her chest and dresser. All her silverware was there, as well as toothpaste, dishes, coffee, bank statements dating to the 1950s, and pictures of the grandchildren. Also I found a partial sack of vanilla wafers, telephone books, Bibles, several shoes (no two that matched), and her Depression glass items, each piece wrapped in my stepfather's boxer shorts. A hundred other things, all unrelated and out of context, hidden away to keep others from "stealing them."

The purse was not among them, however. It was not under the bed, but back issues of the *Cleburne Times Review*, dating to World War II, were well represented there. Neither was it in her trunk, where I found more toothpaste, boxes of tea, hair rollers, a portable radio, and, also wrapped tightly in Raymond's shorts, her television clicker.

Finally, in the bottom of an overnight bag along with more dishes, washer detergent, and an ancient box of Toni permanent solution, I found the purse. She had dropped out of the search after only a few seconds. She had found a batch of old family photos. We were due at the dentist's office in twenty minutes, and she was rhapsodizing about Grandma Overton's pretty smile.

"Where are we going?" she says, as we drive west toward Joshua.

"To the dentist. You have to get a tooth pulled."

"Doctor Bell is a good dentist," she says.

"We're not going to Doctor Bell," I say.

"Doctor Bell always pulled Daddy's teeth. He called him a tooth-dentist."

"We're not going to Doctor Bell."

This time, it registers on her. "Well, just turn around and go back!" she says. "I'm not going to any dentist but Doctor Bell."

"Doctor Bell has been dead for forty years."

She gazes out the window as we turn at a little place called Egan. "Egan!" I say, like a train conductor. It is her cue. I know what she's going to say, but I never get tired of hearing it.

"I was born at Egan. Way off out there in the brush. Mama said those were hard old times. Howard took the measles and died when he was just sixteen months old. I was just a month old and slept in the same bed with him. It's a wonder I didn't get them too. Daddy was still sick with the typhoid fever, but he walked all the way up to the Galt's house and called the doctor in Joshua. The baby died before he could get there in his wagon. Uncle Dock was killed in the war not too long after that. They're all buried right out here at Caddo."

On the way back she said, "There's a hole in my gum."

"Yes," I said.

"My tooth is gone."

"Yes," I said.

"I pushed it out with my tongue."

I no longer try to explain things to her. This was one of the hardest lessons to learn about Alzheimer's disease. If she believes she pushed the tooth out with her tongue, then it is better to let it go.

Another hard lesson to learn was that it is less stressful for both of us to let her keep her things hidden. I used to put things back where they belonged, but she only hid them again. So now, I leave them wrapped in Raymond's shorts. We have fun now that I understand she is not of this world anymore, but of the world of Times Past.

And I believe she thinks she's going back there any day now, and must stay packed and ready to go.

· · · 🐾 · · ·

# Shepherds Abiding in the Lawns

I have little or no appreciation for the modern trend of Christmas light displays for homes and lawns. I realize that it's an ancient ritual designed to combat winter's darkness, but I also know that things will lighten up again. By the time June gets here, we will have all the daylight we can stand. I don't think it is religious anymore. I believe that status is involved. It is a law of status that whatever is proven to attract attention will always be exaggerated until it becomes grotesque. Small feet are attractive—okay, we have foot binding. Women with long, swan-like necks are pleasing. Get out the neck rings. The neighbors light up their window at Christmas. We outline our house. And so on.

I've heard about magnificent displays from my friends who drive throughout the city to see them. They have even invited me to come along so that I might see them and improve. I have two jogging buddies who go on annual jogs through Dallas' Highland Park area to behold the splendor as they simultaneously honor Onus, the god of jogging.

I know things change, but I remember Christmases when everybody's house at night didn't look like Caesars Palace. We strung lights on a tree and put it in the window. Merchants put lights in their storefronts, and the courthouse was lit up at night. But the topic of climbing up on the roof and stringing lights along the eaves never came up at our house. Number one, my grandfather was a little too weary after a hard day at the railroad shopyard to go up on a ladder when he came home. And number two, he would have considered this idea an extravagant waste of "juice," his word for electricity. He had a rule of thumb about this: Never get on the roof unless you're patching a leak or adjusting the television antenna. My grandmother considered it unladylike to get on the roof for any reason.

This may sound melodramatic, but the lights I liked in those days were in the Milky Way. I remember those Christmases when, on clear and crisp nights, the stars were so spectacular that you couldn't help but think of how one of these same stars pointed the way to the birthplace of the Prince of Peace. The night sky on Christmas Eve was a sight so spectacular and so grand that even a thoughtless child was filled with wonder and the hope of peace on earth and good will toward all people.

Now, the city's bright lights and the lights of suburban status-seekers have all but obliterated this star-spangled vision of my childhood Christmas. Rather than look heavenward on Christmas, people look to their neighbors' lawns, outlined with store-bought lights.

In the Silver Creek Crossing neighborhood in DeSoto, residents receive a flyer each year instructing them on the proper specifications for house and yard light displays. "Purchase 18-inch wooden stakes from Home Depot," these residents are told. The stakes are to be driven into the ground at two-and-a-half-foot intervals. "You will need miniature white lights," the instructions say, which are to be attached to the stakes "with staple guns or tacks...from top to top." Each light must be exactly ten inches from the ground. And since the lights may be displayed only from 5:30 P.M. to 10:30 P.M., December 4 through 26, residents are told to get automatic timers to insure synchronized displays. Painting the stakes is, mercifully, optional.

Diagrams embellish these instructions to further prevent deviations. The flyer does not specify the punishment for failure to abide by these instructions. Personally, I wouldn't want to find out.

Again, I know that things change. But it is awfully hard for me to accept the modern assumption that peace and good will can be reduced to a matter of inches and the heavenly hosts bought at Home Depot.

· · ·  · · ·

# 1998

*We are the shrink-wrapped, zip-locked generation.*

## Sack and Save

When horror rained down on Buddy Halyard, pain eventually became his only companion. He said he couldn't see, feel, or hear anything but the pain.

I met him in Fort Worth at the home of Richard Rogers, another classmate, to engage in the higher forms of reminiscence—mostly involving our won-loss record in the game of high school romance. Soon, I became bored with these statistics. I wanted to hear the story of how Buddy overcame the horror.

Buddy and I were roommates in college. Though the same number of years have passed for him as for me, he is one of those people who grow old slowly. He was good-looking in college and could get the girls, and he still is and still can. Good hair and teeth, skin, and sense of humor still intact. Unpretentious as ever.

He had been an aeronautical systems illustrator for various companies, including NASA, when he decided to retire rather than swap his drawing nibs for a computer mouse. Retirement alone can take some getting used to, but it was minor compared with the whams that life sent his way at this time. His sister died and her husband too. She was his only sister, and her husband was as a brother to him. Also during this period, Buddy's son and wife of thirty years died.

Whether he was next was a matter of no concern to him for a long time after that. But he slowly recovered enough to start going outside again, even dating. After a few false starts, he met the right woman and they became inseparable. They went places, laughed, were kids again. At sixty, Buddy was in love. They were going to get married. There was no question about that. He was on top of the world.

When the dread call came, it didn't really register on him: "Old boyfriend came to town. It wasn't planned. I'm sorry." It was over.

"I sat outside her work just hoping for a glimpse of her when she came out," he said. "I called her. Begged. Cried. I did all the humiliating things. It was awful."

This was the Sunday punch that sent Buddy Halyard down to the canvas. All the other horrors had set him up and when this punch came, he could hardly hear the ten count. He was out.

For months he stayed at home and drank and cried, paced, cried some more, kept on drinking. He lost weight, thought he was dying. He didn't care.

A former work friend heard about his travails and called him. He asked if he could come over. "I didn't want him to, but I said yes," Buddy said. "I'm glad I did. He told me he knew what I was going through because he had been there. He wanted me to know there was hope. He had a nice wife now and was happy. So, I guess that had an effect on me."

A psychiatrist had helped him, and he recommended him to Buddy. Buddy went, but reluctantly. He told Buddy that he would prescribe the usual mood elevators, but he also had another suggestion. He wanted Buddy to get some kind of job, any job, but preferably one with people around.

He stopped at the grocery store on the way home and noticed that the man sacking groceries was older than he was. "I applied and they hired me and I started the next day," he said. After a month I threw away the pills. I still had crying jags, but when I did I'd go round up buggies on the parking lot until I got over it. After six months I was a new man."

The new man now has a new woman. She lives in Hillsboro. They go places, have fun, laugh. At sixty-two he's a kid again. He's in love, on top of the world.

Go Buddy Go!

· · · 🌰 · · ·

## The Coneys of No Change

Pampa's Coney Island Café is one family-owned café in Texas that the fast-food chains have been unable to intimidate and run out of business. Brothers John and Ted Gikas have been the geniuses behind the grill on West Foster Street since 1952, and before that it had been owned and operated by their uncle, Bill Coronis. He came from Greece and started ladling the chili and cheese here in 1933. It has been open six days a week ever since, year round, except for the last week of May and the first two weeks of June. Ted goes to Greece and John rests.

From eleven A.M. to seven P.M., their devoted customers fill the small wooden booths and the twenty-two stools along the counter to dine on the delectable coneys (80 cents), cheeseburgers (1.40), sandwiches and stew, and seventeen varieties of pie (80 cents), made fresh each morning. John usually makes the pies and Ted the chili, twenty pounds daily. Forget the pale and generic, characterless bucket-brigade burgers assembled by indifferent teenagers and served on Styrofoam plates. At the Pampa Coney Island Café, the brothers Gikas personally prepare each of the twelve menu items fresh daily. Thankfully, nothing has changed since their uncle's day except prices (still unbelievably low), the refrigeration system, and the addition of stew to the menu.

Nobody's saying there's anything wrong with change. But it's disheartening to see office buildings and the like going up virtually overnight where old and familiar landmarks stood for years. Developers cement over childhoods and brick up memories, and tradesmen transact deals on the spot where, as teenagers sighing like furnaces, we transacted romantic, back-seat business in the ever-receding memory of adolescent moonlit nights. We all love an unchanged delight. The poet Mark Strand calls this happy sentiment the "meat of memory, the meat of no change," symbolized in one of his poems by his mother's changeless pot roast.

I returned to Pampa after many years for my own taste of the meat of memory. I spent some of my best adolescent years here. This would be the early 1950s, when Pampa's mighty Harvesters dominated Texas high school basketball. These titans dined on coneys each schoolday at lunch, and I rushed down there to see them as they came in. Gary Griffin, Ken Hinkle, E.J. McIlvain, and Jimmy Bond—they were like gods, just a few stools away, wolfing down the Gikas brothers' unbeatable, championship coneys.

Driving through Pampa these many years later, I pass the spot where my old junior high used to be—it's a drive-in bank now. Downtown, where retail stores once were, the town sells its memories in antique stores. The oil and gas bust of the 1980s reduced its population by 6,000. What fresh hell awaits at 114 West Foster? I wonder. At the courthouse, I turn and go one block and—there it is: the sign says Pampa Coney Island Café!

I sit on one of the same stools I sat on as a boy and place my order. "Three coneys on one, custard!" sings out the waitress, Pam Best. She's thirty-eight and supports herself and four children on her salary. Lisa Bowers has been calling out orders since she was fourteen.

Ted hears their orders over the great din but reacts only by rolling the weiners and slapping meat on the grill. He extracts buns from the warmer (the same one used by Uncle Bill) and brushes on the chili and mustard (there's a correct consistency for optimum spreading) and sprinkling on the onions. She brings my order on real plates, then returns to Ted or John with the money. No one else goes into the cash register.

Ted, less talkative than John, prefers the solitude of the grill, which he plays like some kind of culinary keyboard; only the smoky music he makes soothes the savage palate. It is an almost continuous moment of meat-sizzling, weinie-grilling, bun-splitting, chili-and-mustard-ladling, onion-showering rhapsody.

When there's a lull, John socializes with the customers. When he was six years old in the neighbor town of Borger, he says, he hawked newspapers in Greek, the only language he knew. After particularly bloody nights when there had been several killings, he sold lots of papers, sold them all night when the sheriff was shot. His hard-working parents, Nestor and Aphrodite Gikas, needed the extra money.

"Bob Wills stopped by one night to show his band where he washed thousands of dishes during the Depression. John sometimes takes customers next door and shows them the bricked-up doorway where the future bandleader once cut hair before trading his comb and scissors for a fiddle and bow.

Speaking of stories, John enjoys talking about the times he had with Woodie Guthrie, who used to hang out at the Coney

Island Café in the days after World War II. Woodie even wrote a song about the place, "All Alone on Saturday Night."

These are great stories, but they're John's memories. Mine, though less renowned, are gladdening nonetheless. I turn suddenly and half-expect to see the hungry Harvesters come bounding through the door.

They didn't, of course, but I didn't care. I had tasted the coneys of my childhood, the pie of memory, "the meat of no change."

. . . 🦃 . . .

## What's a Three-Letter Word Meaning Anger

Well, that would be *ire*. In this case, it means the emotion caused by messing with the crossword puzzle.

The *Dallas Morning News* received multitudes of calls and letters recently containing mild oaths (egad) and perhaps some biblical curses (raca) from area puzzle fans when the paper suddenly and without warning altered the daily Tribune Syndicate crossword puzzle. The paper wanted to reflect, it said, "the eighties and nineties." To most puzzlers, this may as well have been a death knell (peal) for their morning routine (habit). The paper might as well have thrust a dagger (snee) through their hearts.

Puzzlers don't care very much about the eighties and nineties; if they did they would be watching television instead of working the puzzle. "Reflecting the eighties and nineties" really means, I suspect, "reflecting the tastes of baby boomers," the large demographic group who buy most of the products advertised in the paper. Also, the change coincided with the replacement of the eighty-one-year-old puzzle editor by one who was forty-nine. Age forty-nine means baby boomer. Hence, all the new references to the Brady Bunch, the fashion industry, and other aspects of popular culture. Puzzlers consider pop culture a vast wasteland (common) and something to avoid (eschew).

Before this debacle (breakdown) occurred, I worked this puzzle with great enjoyment (elation). Suddenly, I couldn't work it at all. I had never heard of these television celebrities and rock stars. I could not recall the name of the guitar player for the Rolling Stones. All I knew was that he was very ugly.

I made a frantic call to my old pal and puzzle expert (mavin), Richard Rogers, in Fort Worth. He works the *New York Times* puzzle—even on Sunday! To get me started as a puzzler a few years before, he had made me a list of words that were old and obscure (arcane), words commonly used in most puzzles. "I don't get it!" I said. "I can't even work the Monday puzzle. That list you gave me is useless now." The knowledge that a bird's beak is a *neb*, that Fred Astair's sister is *Adele*, or that Guido's high note is *ela*, was as useless as a Japanese banjo (samisen).

I believe he suggested that I say a prayer to the dawn goddess (Eos)—or maybe he told me to go soak my flax (ret)—I don't recall. I told him that whoever is responsible for this had better head for shelter (alee) fast because I can imagine the word-lovers (logophiles) shouting something that sounds like a Bacchanalian war cry (Evoe!).

Oh brother, did they ever shout. Nothing gets people more worked up than fiddling with their habits. Blackie Sherrod (*Morning News* Sports Page Icon) wrote only a few months ago these immortal words: "Don't mess with my crossword puzzle." And durned if they didn't go and do it anyway. Blackie's warning should have been taken seriously, but people seem not to listen to their elders anymore. They should, because heeding could save them from stepping into an abyss (chasm). In Blackie's day, mine, too, when a tribal elder said, "Don't mess with my crossword puzzle," you naturally looked for something else to mess with. This is a custom (more) those under fifty should acknowledge for their own good.

Our warnings should be heeded because very few things ever happen for the first time. We could have warned President Clinton (baby boomer) not to place his wife in charge of developing a national health care system or to state publicly that he intended to legalize homosexuality in the military. Blackie's generation remembers that President Roosevelt (older and wiser) relied on his own wife but did so in an unofficial manner. Those of my own generation remember how easily an older President Truman quietly finessed integration into the military and instigated (fomented) no controversy doing it. But as with the paper's messing with the crossword puzzle, President Clinton did not ask for our opinion.

We may be out of date (anachronism) but we have a comparative point of reference (perspective). If we're not interested in the latest popular movie or television comedy show, it's because it's probably an imitation (counterfeit) of something we might not have liked very much the first time. We're more interested in Captain Ahab than Captain Crunch. We may not know much about the Brothers Menendez, but we're informed (hep) on the Brothers Karamazov. Hootie and the Blowfish may leave us cold, but we know a conger (eel) when we see one.

As it turned out, the eggy-faced editors did a lot of retreating (crawfishing) and promising never to make such a blunder (messing with Blackie's crossword puzzle) again.

The old puzzles are back, and the peace goddess (Irene) rules over all.

# The Jilting of Katherine Anne Porter

There is a house in a small town in Texas where a classic author lived. Katherine Ann Porter was born at Indian Creek in 1890 and grew up in a small frame house in Kyle, twenty miles south of Austin. At twenty, she left Texas and never lived here again.

Her stories are ironic, highly stylized, finely textured, and worldly. They have nothing to do with the Texas myth of cowboys and cattle trails. She has been shamefully unrecognized in this state. Another writer named Porter who spent time in Texas, William S. (O. Henry) wrote a book about cowboys, and his house has been a shrine in Austin for many years.

She is the author of "Pale Horse, Pale Rider," "Noon Wine," "Flowering Judas," and "The Jilting of Granny Weatherall." These are world classics and studied by college students of the past fifty years who have had to take tests over them. Her only novel, *Ship of Fools*, also a literary classic, was number one on the *New York Times* Best Seller list for twenty-six weeks in 1962. In 1966 her collected stories won the Pulitzer Prize.

Yet her childhood house in Kyle wasn't even marked until it was bought by David and Yana Bland and turned into a small museum and community center. Due to their work, the Hayes County Preservation Association, with the aid of donors, has arranged for the house to be restored. Southwest Texas State University will then administer it for public use. Tom Grimes is an author and directs the writing program at the university. He says the plan is to bring the house to its original state and select a writer in residence each year to live there and work with Texas schoolchildren. The funds needed to do this will come from private donors; in other words, from those who want Texas to be known for something loftier than Super Bowl champions and prison construction.

I understand that someone who believes in these things can also believe in the preservation of the arts, but it is a fact that Texans spend more money on season tickets each year for games and more tax money on the crime industry than on the arts. In the daily press yesterday, I read that a third of all Texans can't read the label on a medicine bottle. I believe that education, not prison construction, reduces crime.

Some say the situation is hopeless when three million people in your state can't read well enough to take medicine. Yet, two-thirds can read, not only a medicine bottle label, but they can read books and support projects such as this one.

That Katherine Anne Porter is virtually unknown in Texas symbolizes the state's educational problems. I fight the urge to blame only sports and celebrity fanaticism and TV-addicted parents for the state's grim illiteracy rate. The schools come in for their share of blame. Conventional-minded, overpaid administrators place too much emphasis on controlling students' dress and other fads and not enough on critical thinking and scholarship. Profit-driven textbook publishers cave in to fundamentalists who wish to rewrite history and science.

Katherine Ann Porter's ship of fools would have to be a much larger vessel today.

· · · ❦ · · ·

## We're Geezers But Not Wheezers

I like railroads and the outdoors. I also like fellow geezers John (March or Die) Tushim, Floyd (Doc) Keen, and Jon (Bunky)

McConal. Jon has been a Fort Worth *Star-Telegram* columnist since the Coolidge administration, I think. He wanted us to be his troops, along with Tipper, my golden retriever, for his assault on the Lake Mineral Wells State Trailway, a twenty-three-mile hike between Weatherford and Mineral Wells.

We began at Grace Cartwright Park on Farm Road 920 near Weatherford. The trail was formerly a railway line, and every now and then you can still see the tracks beneath the trail.

With the weight of routine problems in abeyance, we stepped lightly into the morning air. The path stretched out before us like hope, the kind you had when you were young and didn't know any better. Suddenly, we were boys again, walking down the railroad line going somewhere as boys do just to be going.

Mustang grapevines coiled along the fence rows, and black-berry vines flowered at our feet. The pastures alongside bloomed in vivid hues of orange and yellow and blue. Tipper felt so frisky that he jumped on a junkyard dog out on a morning stroll. Doc, a veterinarian, separated them with a cudgel, none too soon to suit Tipper. He was bitten as badly as if he had been in the ring with Mike Tyson. "He loved it, don't worry," Doc said. "Animals challenge themselves all the time. People should too."

Around Doc's campfire that night, we geezered well into the morning hours, attentive to his theories on Italian women and how they lifted American morale during World War II. Doc, who allowed Patton to help him take Italy, was the ranking geezer on World War II. Tushim, veteran of the Korean War, regaled us with his five-star quality meatballs and spaghetti and a running commentary on the ordnance specifications of every weapon ever fired anywhere on the planet.

In keeping with Doc's warning that we need to challenge ourselves more, I suggested "March or Die" as a possible national motto. Because, as Bunky pointed out, here we were, combined ages 265, two of us over seventy, heart attacks and bypass surgery and cirrhosis of the liver all over our medical charts—out here in the middle of nowhere, marching like infantry. With the zeal of all proselytizers, I said everybody ought to do it. We've become a nation of fearful and sterile thanatosophobes, so terrified of germs and criminals and cults and viruses and liberals that we live behind barred windows and doors and hooked up to alarm systems. We drink bottled water and eat food stripped of all taste and character. Instead of walking and riding bikes, we travel in locked cars, our cell phones at the ready and our thumbs on 911. We are the shrink-wrapped, zip-locked generation.

Come morning, Commandant Bunky pointed at a spot on the trail map and said, "Boys, here's where we are now, and here's where we have to go." A blister, a hiker's nightmare, had come up on my heel the day before, but I challenged myself and marched ever onward. Pain, I told myself, is a positive emotion and is necessary for us to know pleasure. I talked to the blister in a friendly manner and welcomed it along on the trip. The others thought I was delirious and tried to make me drink water.

But I was fine. As anyone would be who had made the trek along the Lake Mineral Wells State Trailway, with forays into philosophy, war, and a dogfight's deeper meanings.

## Johnson County Dreamin'

At the Cafe Aspen in Fort Worth I am eating baked salmon and mixed vegetables. It's okay, if you like elegant regale. I'm with Don Siratt, and he likes fine cuisine now. Once upon a time, we were poor together. I still call him Donnie.

He lived in Grandview but came to Cleburne regularly, as that was where the pretty girls were. There were pretty ones in Grandview, but we had more of them. Since Donnie's father worked at a two-pump filling station in Grandview, he could get away with telling the Cleburne girls that his father was an oilman.

He didn't follow his father into the oil business. He went to work at the Texas and Pacific Railroad in Fort Worth, which is where I worked. Since we were laid off so much, we were, once again, poor together. During those long third-shift train yard nights of hostling engines to and from the depot, we talked about our dreams. We had wives by then and small children. We had plans and provisions to seek a world elsewhere. I was already taking college courses by day. "You should too," I told him.

"I'd love to have an education," he said. "But I'd rather be rich, and I will be someday."

Our worlds elsewhere seemed on the other side of the moon, though. But then a great thing happened. We got fired.

The railroads laid off all their firemen in 1964 and gave us severance pay. I used mine to finish college. He opened a small appliance store in Fort Worth and bought an old delivery truck. We bought a color TV from him. Xerox paid him fifty dollars every time he delivered a copy machine, and he gave me ten for helping. Once, the front wheel almost fell off, and the fifty went for a new wheel bearing.

Soon, he was back on the road, this time in Dallas, with several trucks and a dozen employees. He had his own company, Western Transfer Service. I was teaching at Mountain View College nearby. One day he picked me up at the college in a limousine driven by a beautiful woman in uniform. He and his Rolex watch were in the back seat. I looked around, hoping no one saw me get in. "You're not impressed, are you?" he said.

That was twenty years ago. I look across the table at him now. The massage and facial he gets each week apparently work. He looks ten years younger than he is. He's trim and muscular from working out, his skin unlined and pink as his grandbaby's behind. His hair is intact and every one in its place. The owner of the café calls him Mr. Siratt and appears to genuflect. He gets such deference because, true to his word, he has made more money than he could spend in ten lifetimes.

He gives much of it away now—for college scholarships, homes for unfortunate children, homeless shelters, causes of all kinds that are sponsored by his wife, Gloria. Last year he heard that Happy Hills Farm, a facility for children with cancer, needed a bus. He bought them a new sixty-seat, top-of-the-line Bluebird bus and asked the headmaster not to publicize it. He has done many other good things with his money. I have taught over seven thousand students to read and write better, but the results are not so readily apparent as the sight of sixty happy children waving appreciatively from the windows of their new Bluebird bus.

He lives less ostentatiously than he once did. Gone are the Rolls Royces, Porsches, Rolexes, Jaguars, and limos. He and his wife live in an apartment in downtown Fort Worth and have a ranch west of Weatherford. He still has plans and provisions, though. He hopes to sell his business and open an office downtown where he can concentrate on his charities. Next to his own five children, the children he helps are most important to him. He knows, of course, something of deprivation.

Though my teaching days are over, I tell him, I have my own plans, some of them yet undreamed. "I'm not through yet," I say. "I hope to write more books before repairing to the marble orchard."

Here we are, I thought. Two Johnson County boys, still dreaming, still learning. If I have made him less suspicious of "liberals," he has shown me that nothing, not even riches, can turn a good man bad.

· · · 🐂 · · ·

# In the Beginning Was the Word But the Word Now is Profits

If the news weren't bizarre enough, comes now a story on "specialty Bibles." There's the Men's Devotional Bible. There's the long-awaited Promise Keepers' Men's Devotional Bible. Of course, you have your Senior's Devotional Bible and, for women, the Woman's Devotional Bible.

Then, wouldn't you know it? You have your Mom's Bible, your Couple's Bible, and your Believer's Bible. This is the gospel truth.

I still like the King James Version but see no reason why there shouldn't be others. In fact, why not a Texas Man's Bible? I can easily imagine what it would be like for, say, the 23rd Psalm:

*The Lord is my buddy, we hang together*
*And go hunting and to the ball games and stuff.*
*He's with me at the lake and even at the deer lease.*
*He keeps me on the straight and narrow and out of dutch*
*With the little woman.*
*Talk about your valley of the shadow of death, hey,*
*I've been in some serious scrapes, now.*
*But I'm not a bit scared 'cause the Big Guy is with me*
*And He packs some heavy artillery, you know what I'm saying?*

Of course, there would have to be a Texas women's version—which might be rendered after this wise:

*The Lord is my companion, y'all;*
*We have a meaningful relationship*
*That is based on trust and sharing.*
*He maketh me to lie down in bluebonnets*
*And have my picture taken. He leadeth me*
*To sit beside the fountain waters at the shopping mall.*
*He restoreth my soulmate.*
*My soulmate runneth over every time I call.*
*I'm not afraid of death 'cause I know He's there for me.*
*But I wish He'd send me a cure for wrinkles in my lifetime.*

And, of course, there would have to be a Bureaucrat's Bible.
How would a bureaucrat handle the Lord's Prayer? Something
like this, maybe:

*Our Father Figure, who resides in the upper-echelon domain,*
*May thy title always be structured to elicit a favorable response.*
*Reward us today, bread-wise,*
*And minimize our unfavorable self-concept resulting from*
*credit over-extension,*
*As we will endeavor to practice reciprocal procedures.*
*And channel us not into temptation-inducing areas*
*But provide us with security from situations not conducive*
*to moral enrichment.*
*For thine is the position of maximum achievement in the*
*power structure,*
*Not to mention the prestige-attainment factor that never*
*terminates.*

So, you've got your men's and women's Bibles, your Texan's,
your bureaucrat's, and so on; maybe there ought to be a teenager's Bible. If there were, would the Book of Genesis sound
like this:

*In, like, the beginning? God made the world and everything?*
*At first it was all dark and icky? With everything like, gooey?*
*So God goes, he goes, "Let there be, like, light?"*
*And then He goes, "Cool," and kinda like, waved his hand?*
*And made the sky and water and land and everything?*
*Then, when He made the stars? He goes, "Hmm, all it needs*
*Is a cute couple to be, like, in love? Forever and ever?"*

I'm like, maybe even the most profit-driven of publishers won't go this far? And maybe there are enough of us who still think the King James translation could never be improved, even by, like, Texas English?

· · · ❦ · · ·

## Rockport's Guru of Granite

The sculpted stone monuments of Jesùs Bautista Moroles stand in silent eloquence in galleries and public gardens throughout the country. Soon, they will be in China. One, *Spirit Columns*, stands between the bays at Rockport Beach in the small fishing town of Rockport where he lives and works. It is a rare prophet who is appreciated in his own village.

Monuments co-exist side by side with high-tech computers in the Moroles headquarters. Here, two-dozen employees and uncountable mercantile details are monitored and coordinated by his eagle-eyed, protective sister, Susanna. These details have accrued from the mundane necessities of payroll to the finer logistics of scheduling the artist's exhibits and workshops, and selling enough of his work to keep such a large operation going.

His work fills every available space—in corners on work desks, on top of file cabinets. Some pieces, like *Vanishing Edge Round,* a notched, leaf-like encurvatured spire of black granite, are privately owned but remanded to their creator for temporary exhibition. Others, like *Texas Stele,* a convex, notched and striated sheet of Texas pink granite, are unsold veterans of the show tour, returned home to wait patiently like unadopted children.

Still others standing about in adorning repose are fresh from the Moroles parturition chamber, newly torn from the granite birthing crotch by giant drills and eighty-pound pneumatic hammers and steel wedges, then sliced and notched by electric circular bridge saws with diamond blades. They will emerge in new form, according to the artist's skilled vision.

The man at the center of all this industry is pictured everywhere, with important personages of wealth and status, even with Hillary Clinton who, in another photo, embraces Jessica, the ten-year-old heir to a fortune of art.

Jesùs Bautista Moroles micro-manages his corporation of art with a genius equal to the making of it. Every telephone conversation is summarized and logged for his perusal. Every press report, article, critique ever written about him is archived. He knows the whereabouts of every piece he has ever sold. By telephone, he masterminds the Rockport operation regardless of where he is in the world. He seems always to know what his workers are doing in the shop. At the core of the shop operation are a few Hispanic men, drilling, sawing, hammering the stone. They have been trained by the artist to execute his wishes, possibly even to know his thoughts.

The genius of Moroles extends to his understanding of the power of myth, not only in the art's making but also in its marketing. He has pointedly avoided mixing issues with his art, saying he is not political except when it comes to his name. In his press kit there is a strict admonition against printing it in part or without the accent mark. He is proud of its defining legacy, he goes on, and speaks contemptuously of "Jesse," an anglicized echo from the past. Call him this and his tone turns dangerous: "This is what people from my past call me who want to bring me down." It is not a warning to take lightly.

Though he makes magnificent art, he knows he must sell Jesùs Bautista Moroles. His name is not only personal and political but, like everything else about him, part of the Moroles mystique. He directs reporters toward the biographical material that forms the myth—of his work in the quarries and studios of Italy where Michaelangelo toiled, of his study in Paris, of his apprenticeship with the great figurative artist Luis Jimenez, of his belief in the spiritual properties of granite. All more or less true, but retold and reprinted so many times that they pass beyond fact into the realm of myth. It is the recurring metaphor of the many published articles inside his big notebook of acclaim. Reporters are also tools of his art. He uses them skillfully to fashion the monument that is Jesùs Bautista Moroles. "I never read anything written about me," says the mythmaker. But someone assuredly does, and the articles are assiduously categorized and archived.

At forty-eight, he is still driven toward success. He is always working. Only sleep, a biological imposition, and city ordinances can silence his saws and hammers. A notebook, frayed with use and heavy with sketches and ideas, is always with him. He himself has become a monument, the artist as art. Years of hefting the stone have developed him into a structure of bone and bulk and muscle. He is dusky from the intense sunlight of the Texas Gulf Coast. He can be soft and sensual, like flowers, but his temperament is intractable as granite. He is sociable with strangers but only in the context of the art. After nearly two decades in

Rockport, he knows but few people here. He has never even seen the whooping cranes. A wife from the early years in Dallas and another woman in Houston can doubtless tell sad stories of the isolation of the artist and of sacred vows made only to granite

A small hallway leading away from the rattling keyboards opens into a kitchen area where *Concave Stele* and *Moonring,* looking like a sea god's pronged scepter, stand facing a gigantic table with a four-inch-thick, five-thousand-pound marble top. In the corner is *Vanishing Edge Round.*

A heavy stone stairway leads to the artist's sitting room, *Texas Stele* waiting at the top, as old Picasso peers, God-like, over a row of art books. In the adjoining bedroom, a bed with three rounded headpieces of solid mahogany, a fine guitar from Spain, signed and framed photos of other famous artists, a large boxed set of enlarged details from *Guernica.*

The complex comprises several large lots on Sixth Street, on Rockport's rural south side. It is modest ground for someone who could easily afford to ensconce himself and his family in one of the seaside mansions in Rockport's Key Allegro section overlooking the bay. José Moroles, father of the artist, bought the property, thinned out the oaks, and with no experience in carpentry, designed and built the uniquely beautiful yellow and white two-storey house of concrete blocks. The son came, and the two of them with the skill of their hands formed the lavish compound.

Behind the house of the senior Moroles is an immense above-ground concrete pool edged in heavy stone blocks designed to look like an ancient ziggurat. It could have adorned the palace of an Aztec king. Father and son are proud of the blood of Montezuma's children that swells their veins. "Jesùs has the look of the Aztec; you can see in his features the features of the Aztec," says the father. His art, too, as that of the Aztec, is sanguinary, is even stained with the blood of his lacerated hands.

A four-thousand-pound table made from the inverted stump of a thousand-year-old oak accommodates the entire Moroles family at once. Running about the orchard of grapefruit, lemon, and nectarine trees are three German shepherd dogs and sixty peafowl. Sitting on the edge of the pool is one of a pair of three-hundred-pound oyster shells. The other is a wash bowl in the artist's bathroom. "Jesùs has the power to put a thing in the air and turn it around and look at it from all sides," says the father. "I too can do this. We do not need computers to do this." The son's myth is of no concern to him. How better to get to the son than through the father?

Between the house and the studio-gallery, the father stands beneath a two-inch iron pipe trellis of flowering grapevines, potato vines, and palmettos. "Jesùs has from birth the gift of art," he goes on. "When he was in fifth grade, his art teacher came to our house and told us she would no longer charge for his lesson and that she would provide all his supplies." Together, he said, teacher and student painted the mural at the Bronco Bowl on Fort Worth Avenue in Dallas.

In the serenity of the moment, he tells the story of himself as a fatherless child in Mexico, of rending poverty, of leaving school in third grade to work, of a child who could have been a sculptor but was forced by economics to grind eyeglass lenses rather than granite. "But it is like art. The lenses must be polished and it must be of a precision," he says.

He and Mrs. Moroles are celebrating their fiftieth year of marriage. They met in Corpus Christi, where a harried border guard took him in 1947 after wearying of deporting him—twenty-seven times. "I wanted to be an American," he said. They have made a family of good citizens. Jesùs Bautista Moroles makes deathless art. Susanna coordinates the business. Hilario, brother of the artist, oversees the shop and works with galleries.

Inside the shop, hydraulic hammers clatter. Diamond-blade saws sing like amplified cicadas. Pulleys and cranes carry three-ton slabs of Marble Falls granite through the air. The stone is drilled with diamond bits; pins are inserted and ratcheted down, finely tuned like strings on a Spanish guitar. The father says the stone is alive. "When it splits, if you put your ear to it, you can hear it cry out." Put another way, it is the sweet song of commerce.

How has success affected the artist? "Before, I could produce only twenty to thirty pieces," he says. "Now, I have the means to produce two or three hundred. I travel—to Aspen, Santa Fe, to Rhode Island, coming up. Then back to Texas for five fountains for the museum at Irving. I'm going to China, where I will do five pieces. Success means I can be more selective in what I do and where I go. I went to the White House with other artists for the dedication of our work in the First Lady's garden. I took Jessica. She got written up in the *Washington Post.*"

His pieces range in size from *Musical Fish*, sitting on the office work-desk, to *Lapstrake*, the sixty-four-ton, twenty-two-foot-tall monument in New York's CBS Plaza. His most massive, though, is the *Houston Police Officers' Memorial*, spanning 120 by 120 feet, two side-by-side pyramids, one inverted, in honor of Houston's police officers killed on duty.

The mind rocks with irony: There have been many innocent police officers killed. They deserve a monument. But how many young sons of Mexico, like Jose Campos Torres, have died while in police custody in this city for alleged minor offences? Where is their monument?

"I am a model for these poor kids, the ones with the spray cans, as I had models that inspired me," says the artist. "I came from a very poor background, and they can look at me and what I have done and see that they can find their dreams too. I tell them they can do it. Last year, I donated a piece to help take kids off the street, and I go and teach them to work with granite. I had models, and I try to be one for others."

He is heavier, and a lot richer, than he was eighteen years ago when he toiled for a monument company in Waxahachie, making and setting gravestones along with fellow sculptor Bill Pochciol. A Moroles piece in those days could be bought for under five hundred dollars. Now, the smallest brings three thousand. Fifteen thousand is the most popular range, he says, but many are sold at thirty thousand. The monumental pieces and the enormous site sculptures bring enormous fees.

Who can explain the power of myth and art to move people? Inside a file cabinet in the Moroles headquarters, among thousands of other archived materials, is a spiraled notebook, heavy with plastic-encased encomiums penned by the art world's expert interpreters. The meaning of the Moroles stones evades them. Like a poem, a Moroles stone "should not mean, but be."

Eternity is all that is on the face of the sculptures of Jesùs Bautista Moroles. They are no more intellectual than broken sheets of sunlight. Like the art of their making, they are invisible as the stillest water.

· · · 🐛 · · ·

# The Lost Art of Play

For valid reasons, parents of today involve themselves in their children's lives more than parents did in my day. Things have changed. Knowing where your children are helps fight drugs, gangs, and pederasts.

All right. But in their zeal to do everything right, these young parents are unintentionally interfering with children's sovereign right to play on their own. Playing without adults around is training for life and essential for creativity. Allowed to play on their own, kids will make up games of all sorts, with rules and territory and goals. They will mete out punishment for infractions and make all sorts of noises with their mouth. This all means something and is important. Adults don't understand it.

I don't see this happening anymore. Vacant lots where children used to play, away from the interference of adults, are quiet now. Television reports of children being snatched have frightened parents to the point that they feel they can't take their eyes off their children for an instant. As a result, children are forced to have organized fun.

This will not be without its consequences. Once, kids had the right to play or not play sports. They chose up sides for a game and those not wanting to play were umpires and scorekeepers. Those playing could run and jump and swing and catch without parents yelling instructions to them, or could even strike out without feeling that they had ruined their parents' lives. They were free to quit and go home when they felt like it. The game went on with one less player. No big deal.

There's entirely too much of this enforced fun going on nowadays. Kids need adults for food, shelter, and the like, but they can play on their own. By appropriating children's play, adults have taken from them the one thing they can do better than adults. When adults get involved this much, it's no longer play—it's sociology.

Across the alley from my house is the playing field for the Diaper League. In the late afternoon, the Land Rovers and minivans roll in and disgorge these tots, ready to give all on the playing fields for mom and dad. Mom sits on the sideline in a folding chair and chats with other moms. Occasionally, one will put down her Dr Pepper and yell, "Come on Colten, hit somebody! You're not blocking!" Well, Colten is but six or seven, and he doesn't want to hit somebody. He wants to be riding his bike. The other moms take the cue and yell for their little Cody or Josh or Hunter or Dakota to hit somebody too.

In his shorts and ball cap, dad is on the field, bellowing instructions and blowing his whistle like a maniac. In his mind he is Vince Lombardi, and the tiny diaper leaguers scrambling and tumbling at his command are the all-stars of the NFL.

Every now and then a kid starts howling and won't stop. His parents are mortified. The howling kid is banished to the sidelines, whimpering mournfully.

At nightfall the struggles end, and the great massive vehicles load up and rush to McDonald's for supper and more organized and controlled fun on the fenced-in, expertly-planned-and-designed, plasticized playground.

There was an Associated Press story recently about parents in Rio Vista, a little town six miles south of Cleburne. The vice-president of the school board and his wife were reprimanded by the Interscholastic League for abusing an official after the football game in which Rio Vista lost to Milsap. The mom is said to have slapped the official, according to UIL records, and the dad said to have asked him where he lived.

Ball games are not this important. Our little granddaughter Beth Hoover, age six, must have been telling us this when she pulled some kind of one-kid protest demonstration during a soccer game by standing on the field as still as an oil painting. Little Taylor and Josh and Cheyenne were kicking the ball by her as she stood there, refusing to move. Despite the coach's pleadings, she folded her arms and persisted with her demonstration of indifference.

After the game, daughter Karen Hoover said, "Way to go, Beth!" and hugged her. No one knew what pushed Beth over the edge. She didn't say.

Maybe, in her kid-wisdom, she knew it was just a game, and just wanted to get this point across to others. In any case, like Karen, I was proud of her, whatever her reason.

• • • 🦂 • • •

## Good Man of Texas

June Welch is now a part of Texas history. Though he never complained, I suspect he was disappointed that his destiny was not to go down in a blast of musket fire at San Jacinto, Goliad, or the Alamo. It was instead to dwindle away from the ravages of a long, lingering illness.

I knew him first from his radio vignettes in which he told stories about the footnote people of Texas. He loved the unheralded people, those who had done some small thing that was an essential part of something big. I met him in person at the Alamo, where he gave a talk in 1990. He was a man of great physical as well as literary presence. He was over six feet tall and weighed 275 pounds, all muscle and gristle. An album brought out after his funeral had photos of him looking like Adonis in his schooldays at Gainesville High School and at TCU. He once tried out for the screen role of Tarzan.

Heart disease virtually skeletonized him toward the last. But he kept quiet about his former athleticism as others chirped about the miles they ran or reps they did in the gym. He was always mum about his accomplishments. A few weeks before he died, I suggested he come out with a collection of his most popular radio pieces that he had done over the years at KRLD and KAAM. "Gee, Tom," he said, "that's a great idea. Let's think about that." Spoken as always in that soft and genteel manner that made everyone comfortable. After he died, I found on his shelf, among the many other Texas books he had written, a copy of just such a book.

He was no self-promoter—a fine quality for a human being, but a bad one for an author—especially in these days of scant substance and hyperbole. His books are solid and fact-filled. His love of his homeland shines through. No hype necessary. They're about windmills, rivers, droughts, barbed wire, battles, courthouses, fistfights, duels, treaties, land, weather. Most of all, they're about people—people usually short on worldly goods but long on integrity. Rather than suffer the humiliation of competing with books by and about celebrities for the attention of editors, he published them himself. The Yellow Rose Press has one author. June Welch *is* the Yellow Rose Press.

Naturally, such a person should be a teacher, and he was—at the University of Dallas, in Irving. His colleagues Dr. Gene Cutsinger and Dr. John Summerfeltd gave eloquent eulogies for him, as did Dr. Leroy Fenton, his pastor. He was described as a man of learning and of courtly manners. The words *cheerful* and *optimistic* came up a lot. June was a doctor, too, they said, with degrees in English, history, and government, as well as law. He had served in several branches of the military, ending as a lieutenant colonel, and he had been an aide to Lyndon Johnson. He spoke of these attainments only when he was asked. My wife, Brenda, called him "a good man." I've never heard her say such a thing before. She's economical with her praise.

He kept going through his extreme weakness. His wife, Lynda, arranged for him to see his friends often. We were Saturday night dinner partners at the Catfish Plantation in

Waxahachie, where he could get his favorite dish—french-fried pickles. He and I had plans to sit on the bench across from the courthouse and charge tourists a dollar to take our picture. He suggested we would have to be "nekkid" in order to make a sale.

We should have done it. After we got arrested, that would been "Another Vignette From Texas History."

· · · ❦ · · ·

## Gathering for Gladys

Ronnie Dawson is just about the tall hog at the trough of rockabilly music. It's a relatively small trough, but he has a large following among working-class youth who fancy 1950s dress, cars, and music. They worship the postage stamp Elvis. They revere Ronnie because he's pre-Elvis rockabilly, and they know he once played on the same show with Elvis at the Dallas Sportatorium.

Ronnie has stayed a bachelor and lived for forty years in the same north Dallas apartment without a bed. He's tall and slender and women naturally like him but fear competing with his music. "He'll get married when Gladys dies," my laconic wife told me in 1973—Gladys being his mother.

Ronnie's daddy had a band during the 1930s called "Pinky Dawson and the Merrymakers." He died when Ronnie was a teenager, and now Ronnie wants to learn all about his daddy's career. He hoped his mother would tell him, but she never got around to it. She died a few months ago, taking with her all the stories that Ronnie longed to hear. Why she was closed to the subject is a mystery to him.

Though he has slept on the same apartment floor for forty years, Ronnie has his eccentricities. He was determined to orchestrate his mother's memorial service in his own way. "I'm not going to let the church people come in and take over the way they like to do," he said. She had been a member of a church at Cedar Creek Lake where she lived, but Ronnie isn't a church-goer. He was forced to go as a boy and not allowed to do the things boys ordinarily do. He never saw a movie or watched television until he was a teenager. He has bad memories of his brief career at Waxahachie's Assembly of God College. There are other reasons, he says, but these are representative.

Brenda and I went to Gladys' service at the schoolhouse at Nash, a tiny community south of Waxahachie near the place where Ronnie grew up. The school was recently restored with the aid of Denver Pyle, the late movie and television actor who lived at nearby Forreston.

Ronnie and his fiancée, Christi, greeted everyone at the door. A soft breeze swayed the elm trees outside and blew through the open windows. It was warm, but there were plenty of drinks on ice. Family members and friends ate and reminisced about Gladys. Then, Ronnie strapped on his guitar. Accompanied by Mike O'Daniel and Johnnie Todd, he sang "I Saw the Light," "I'll Fly Away," "Just a Closer Walk With Thee," and other of her favorite hymns. These were religious songs, sung by a religious person. If Gladys had been there, someone said, she would have been playing her harmonica and dancing.

Then, Ronnie announced that he and Christi had gotten married.

I looked at Brenda with amazement at her skill for prophecy. She only shrugged.

Women may depart the stage, but their intuition abides forever.

# Those Small Town
# Weird Investment Blues

My ignorance of the stock market is deep and absolute. So quite naturally, I bought stocks.

It was through one of those chain brokerages specializing in small towns, in this case, Midlothian.

Actually, I invested in mutual funds. This isn't exactly high risk, but for me a departure from my natural inclination, which is to watch boxing. "You don't want to outlive your money," warned my broker, a twenty-eight-year-old expert on aging.

I said I would rather like it to come out even, kind of like finishing your sandwich and potato chips at the same time down at Dee-Tee's Diner.

So a couple of years after my investment, I wanted my money to spend on a new wide-screen TV, a subscription to HBO for my boxing delectation, and a retirement chair with a gearshift on the side. "But it's working so well for you," he said. "You've made fifty percent on your investment."

This is a broker's way of saying eleven percent, minus fees.

"But what's the good of it if it isn't in my pocket?" said I.

Leaving without my money, I felt as I used to when my granddaddy turned me down. Except this was my own money!

Eventually, the time came when I needed the money for something even more important. This time my cherubic life advisor said he had no problem with that—meaning "in a pig's eye." He brought up the three percent withdrawal fee. I didn't care. I wanted my money, not a lecture on outliving my money or how well it's working for me. I used some expletives apparently unknown to the curriculum of brokerage school training. They were directed not at him, you understand, but at fate which brought us together.

This is when he told me to get a new broker.

I knew it. I had gone and said something.

So I transferred my account to a neighbor town, Cedar Hill. I was free of this didactic wunderkind, and he could surely rejoice in the departure of a Ludditic geezer intent on outliving his money.

What happened next beat anything.

First, my new broker called and said he would see to it that I got my money in a timely fashion. Oh no, I said, this means I'll never get it.

He called again and said there would be two checks sent but that one of them would be bogus. A woman in St. Louis would be stopping payment on it because I had written a check on my account that hadn't cleared yet.

"There's enough money in that account to cover that check," I said.

"I know," he said. "It's crazy."

His secretary called after that and said they were going to "overnight" me the money from St. Louis and to forget about not cashing the bogus check because they're going to try to locate the woman and stop her from canceling that check.

"I don't want to hear any more of this," I said. "I'm getting a headache."

She called back later and I wouldn't answer. She left a message saying the check-canceling woman could not be found but that the entire amount would be wired to my account by three the next day.

I checked the next day and the money was, incredibly, there.

The next day I received two more checks, signed by Mr. John Bartlett, an unwitting participant in this monetary madness.

It's enough to make you not care whether you outlive your money or not.

# Touring the Cataract Factory

My mother has cataracts, so her doctor referred her to an oph-thalmologist in Burleson. Though this physician had been apprised of her Alzheimer's disease, he nevertheless launched into his usual litany of complicated pre- and post-surgical instructions. My mother smiled at him crookedly and nodded.

There was no time for questions or discussion with this assembly-line man. His assistant would answer all my questions, he told me, before whirling away to his next geriatric paycheck.

His assistant was a high-velocity HMO expert whose function it was to make all the complicated arrangements for insurance payment for the $3,000 surgery. It would occur, along with a full schedule of others, at eight A.M. on a Friday morning in Fort Worth.

She won't be able to give herself the eye drops every hour on the day before surgery and on a regular basis for three weeks thereafter, I told this factotum. She'll wonder why she has an eye patch and throw it away. In order to get her to the surgery site that early, I would have to spend the night with her. The surgery is done one eye at a time, meaning that all these procedures must be done twice, a couple of months of intensive care for which I'm responsible. If I don't do it, then she must go to the nursing home for the pre- and post-surgery care. There are no other alternatives.

I could have added that we have family members who still maintain that she is all right, needs no assisted-living facility, and is perfectly capable of living on her own. They do not volunteer their help on these occasions, however.

She has no one else. I'm the guy.

It is too complicated, I went on. I would literally have to move in with her for six weeks in order to do it.

After days of worry and contemplation, I called off the surgery.

"She already has Alzheimer's," said this HMO liaison factotum. "Why add blindness to her problems?"

Now I'm blinding my mother.

I took her to an optometrist who told me he has seen worse patients. She has quarter vision in one eye and half in the other. Not really correctable, but she no longer drives, reads, writes, dials the telephone, or watches television. She can, however, read road signs with seeming ease, especially those designating her hometown of Cleburne. To her, Cleburne is Eden and if she could but get back there, all would be well. When she lived there, she says, she could remember things; she could keep house; she could drive. It is only since being removed from Cleburne, she thinks, that all these things have happened to her. I drive out of my way for miles to avoid these signs.

Now she has new glasses, the kind with stylish, ultra-light frames. She's happy, and on the lookout for road signs. I escaped the stress of taking her through the cataract factory. Again, this is a safe and worthwhile procedure for those who need it, but for her it wasn't practical. I am prepared to live with my guilt when I make wrong decisions, but even the right ones are not always guilt-free. The care-giving game doesn't come with an instruction booklet.

She sees better now. She stares at the pictures of her grandchildren and great-grandchildren lined up on her wall. "Aren't those pretty children!" she says. "Who are they?"

# 1999

*Great books liberate readers from the bonds of conventional wisdom promoted by the marketplace.*

## Upon What Meat Doth This Our Geezer Feed

When I'm in Cleburne and want to eat food, not dine on cuisine, I go either to Morris Neal's Handy Hamburgers or Chaf-In. Morris Neal died a few years ago, and Handy Hamburgers is now owned by Steve Jones. But the burgers taste the same as they did back in the 1940s and '50s when Morris Neal operated out of a hole in the wall on South Main Street. The place was too small to accommodate inside customers so you had to get your burgers through the alleyway window. People who had cars drove through and picked them up. They were six for a dollar. This may have been the first drive-through establishment.

I like to go there for the old-fashioned burgers and also because I usually run into at least one of my old high schools pals. One, Robert Bilton, manages the place. Last time I was in, we learned that we're going to be neighbors in eternity, as our family plots at Caddo Cemetery near Godley are adjoining. "You're not going to say, 'There goes the neighborhood,' are you?" I said.

"Aw, you're not so bad—compared to some of the other characters out there," he said.

The Chaf-In is still located in its original spot, 209 West Henderson, across from the City Hall and jail. It is named after its founder, Carl Chafin, who still lives in Cleburne. As teenagers we gathered there after dates and ate chicken fried steaks and french fried potatoes, and then went home and went to bed. Though we still meet there occasionally—at an earlier hour—and the wonderful burgers, chicken fried steaks, and pie still taste the same, we pay homage to our viscera by ordering the lunches much more than we used to.

There are two other favorite places that I've been patronizing but a short time, about twenty years. They're in the Oak Cliff section of Dallas. Cooper's, a neighborhood bar and grill at Illinois Avenue and Cockrell Hill, has big tasty hamburgers and small prices. On Wednesday nights I would go down there after class and get their lovely tacos for fifty cents each. It's a blue-collar place and loud sometimes, especially during dart games. There are no tables behind the dartboards.

Once, when I taught at nearby Mountain View College, I went to lunch with the chancellor of the Dallas County Community College, William Wenrich, the boss of bosses. He asked me where I would like to go and I said Cooper's. He called back later and suggested that we meet on his turf, in a penthouse restaurant of some building downtown—I forget the name of it. I said okay and met him there. Though the conversation was good, I felt uncomfortable with the opulence. The food was feckless and cuisiney, and I kept wishing I had held out for Cooper's.

The best place for Mexican food is Tachito's, near the intersection of Illinois and Westmoreland, also in Oak Cliff. When we had guest speakers at the college and wanted to give them the best treatment we took them to Tachito's. Diana Garcia, the original owner, is celebrating its twentieth anniverary this year. It still has that 1970s hacienda look; the food tastes exactly as it always did; and people's heroes Diego Reviera, Pancho Villa, and Emiliano Zapata still glare menacingly from framed pictures on the walls.

These are not restaurants for those desperate to live to a hundred. Camel smokers come in and fire up. Hydrocarbons, carcinogens, and sodium triglycerides have been known to gather here.

But it's actually good for you. Mark Twain explains it: There was a widow woman who never smoked, drank liquor, took snuff, or ate pork. When she got old, she had no way to reform. Poor old soul, he said, a sinking ship and no freight to throw overboard.

I'm making sure that when my time comes for the doctor to tell me to cut back, I won't have to look at him dumbly and say that I have nothing to forego but tofu, skim milk, and celery.

· · · 🐦 · · ·

## The World's Worst Poet

English teachers like odd characters but prefer that they remain between the covers of their anthologies. This is about as close as they want to get to oddballs like Bartleby or Hazel Moats. I believe they would have liked W. K. Hill if they had only read about him in their textbook.

A lot of people think they can be writers, but no one really wanted to be one more than W. K. He seemed to know all the rules of grammar, spelling, and composition. Other than containing more odd fonts than a ransom note, his writing *looked* normal—until you read it. A poem of his was an enigma wrapped in a conundrum. Personally, I preferred a subpoena to one of them. Any poem of his had a misalignment about it—it was like a picture of James Carville hanging crookedly on the wall; you could straighten it up, but it wouldn't improve the picture very much. *Finnegans Wake*, I reminded myself, is incomprehensible to me too. I knew that W. K. was no James Joyce, but he had a similar lunacy about him, common among artists. W. K., I decided, was an artist—just a very bad one.

One of his teachers at Mountain View College, Dr. R. P. Dexter, whose misfortune it was to receive these poems on a regular basis, assessed one by saying: "W. K., if this is not a joke, it may very well be the worst poem ever written." Other such supporters of W. K. included myself, Dr. Paul Benson, and Dr. Geoffrey Grimes. The rest fled seeing him coming.

His long, nicotine-ravaged face and the way he combed his steel-gray hair straight back with broad strokes reminded me of the playwright Samuel Beckett. The resemblance stopped here, however.

W. K. subsisted on cigarettes, black coffee, and day-old pastry foraged from the faculty lounge. He had but six teeth in his chaps and appeared as weak as a vegetarian cat. His double-knit suits were worn almost to the linings, and his shoes were as thin as potato skins. The car he lived in hadn't been licensed or inspected in years. It was a muscle car with abs and pecs that had gone sallow. Its vinyl top appeared to have been buffed by Freddy Krueger. At sixty-nine with no home or family and just a small social security check to live on, he enrolled in graduate school.

I've never known a student more deserving yet so unnerving. He was joyful, polite as an Edwardian doorman, and had more energy than any of his nineteen-year-old classmates. But seeing him coming, armed with poetry, teachers and administrators held their skirts and ran. All women ducked for cover at the first sound of his honking, metallic voice. When he was elected president of Phi Theta Kappa, horrified faculty sponsors nullified the election.

He was deposed but not finished. It took a University of Texas at Arlington English professor to finish him. He drew a line in the chalk dust—either W. K. depart his classroom or else. I empathized with this vexed scholar, encountering one of W. K.'s themes for the first time. You fantasize about other lines of work. A life at sea seems a favorable alternative. Bad grammar is verifiable and is the English teacher's paycheck. It is to the English teacher what crime is to the judge. But W. K., like Mr. McGoo, bumbled across a busy turnpike of grammar laws, always arriving safely on the other side, oblivious to the wreckage he had wrought.

He showed me the tortured professor's comments on the offending theme. The subject was someone named de Saussure, whom W. K. was soon referring to as "de Sausage." The professor's marginalia signaled an impending crackup:

"I'm not even suggesting directions for improvement. I'm just expressing, explicitly, my sense of incomprehension. You clearly don't know what you're talking about . . . yet you don't admit you don't understand; you just write nonsense. . . . Unless everything changes for you in this course, you are headed for failure and should drop as soon as possible."

W.K.'s prose was meaningless, of course, but so was the topic. So, for that matter, is much of what passes for prose in doctoral dissertations. This professor's favorite author, W. K. said, was Emily Dickinson. Something tells me this poet, the oddest in all American literature, would prefer W. K. to this mortarboardsman.

W. K. owned a crypt at Hillcrest Mausoleum in Dallas' heavy-purse section. He bought this in the days when he was up and in, but when he died in 1997 he was down and out, and there was no money to pay for his interment there. His ashes ended up in a good place, though—in a receptacle on Dr. Grimes' desk.

The crypt would have been good, too. His neighbor in perpetuity would have been the Reverend W. A. Criswell, pastor of the First Baptist Church of Dallas. Dr. Criswell is not only a famed defender of the down and out but also a noted interpreter of the Book of Revelation. Anyone who can do that might even have appreciated the perplexing prose and poetry of William Keith Hill.

· · · 🐝 · · ·

## Mother's Day

My mother's telephone rang while she was eating her Mother's Day candy.

We could hear it ringing but couldn't see it. I saw lumps under the bedspread and threw it back. The lumps were the usual items—magazines, Bibles, telephone books, back issues of the *Cleburne Times Review*, several unmatched shoes, framed pictures of her great-grandchildren, an album with no photos, her radio, some spoons wrapped in toilet paper, her television clicker, and half a loaf of Mrs. Baird's bread.

"My birthdays sure come around fast," she said, referring to the candy. She thinks all gifts are birthday gifts.

The telephone was under the bed and had stopped ringing.

We've come to take her to the cemetery to visit her mother's grave. As always, we take the back roads, through Egan. And, as always, she sees the road sign and says what she always says: "I was born at Egan, off out there in the brush. Mama and Daddy took me out there and showed me where it was one time, but I forgot. Tommy knows how to get there."

I'm Tommy.

It's not that she doesn't recognize me. Sometimes, when I go to visit and she's with friends there at the home, she says, "I've got to go; Tommy's here." Then, later, she tells me all about Tommy. The first time she did this I was hurt, but I'm not anymore. I don't understand it, but it must be like that dream we've all had in which we know we're dreaming yet see ourselves in the dream, usually watching the activity.

I've stopped trying to figure it out, and doctors are of little help. It doesn't matter. We talk about Tommy and the bad things he does. She doesn't understand why he and Elvira got married, Elvira being the ninety-three-year-old woman who lives across the hall. "She's bossy and Tommy doesn't like to be bossed," she explains. "It won't last. I give it six months."

She spots the road sign at Joshua and tells me about our relatives there—all dust, of course, but she's in Times Past. When we turn into the entrance to Caddo Cemetery, an aspect of tranquillity moves across her face. She's more at home with the dead than with the living. And they're all there, beginning with her brother, who died in 1918, the year she was born. Next is Uncle Walter, just a teenager, killed by a horse in 1922. Then her Grandma and Grandpa Conner, her parents, another uncle, Tom Conner—all sleeping there together. Adjacent is my stepfather, Raymond. Her name is chiseled on his monument, with the date of death to be added. "I wonder why they left that blank," she always says. "I've got to get them to come out here and fix that."

On the way back, I tell her about her grandchildren. She is shocked that the youngest, Lowell, is thirty. "Even grandchildren get old," I say.

"When we were kids, Daddy worked us so hard we didn't have time to get old," she says.

I couldn't find my camera when we got back. Then I noticed that she was carrying it on her shoulder. "I've got to quit carrying this old heavy purse," she said.

Life can still be fun after Alzheimer's, even if it's among the dead.

· · · ❦ · · ·

# Gainesville's Big Jungle Man

At Cleburne's Santa Fe Elementary, I was so fascinated with a textbook that the principal, J. Pope Koon, gave it to me. I still have it. It is *On Jungle Trails* by Frank Buck, then famous as the jungle man known to "bring 'em back alive." Inside the book are the names of older classmates Jim Easdon and Wanda Rogers, now Land, who still live in Cleburne. I called and asked them if they remembered Frank Buck. No, they said, and they had never heard of *On Jungle Trails*. They were surprised to hear that it had been their textbook. Well, it *has* been a long time.

His fame has died but he was a Texan, born in Gainesville in 1888. As a teenager, he roamed the territory of Plano and Carrollton where my grandfather was born in 1894. I wish I had asked my grandfather if he remembered a boy back then who carried snakes around in his pockets.

I studied this book, especially a photograph of a python that had gone into a cage and swallowed a pig. It was trapped because it was too distended to pass through the bars. It occurred to me at that young age that there are some fixes out of which even the deceitful serpent cannot wriggle.

Further evidence of Buck's eclipse comes from Shana Powell, curator of Gainesville's museum. She learned only recently who he was and that he was from this town. In the time between the two world wars, he was renowned as the pre-eminent adventurer who went into the wild and captured exotic animals, many never seen before. Some he gave names to, as they were yet unknown. To "bring 'em back alive," he crossed the Pacific forty-five times. He would go virtually anywhere, face any danger, surmount any obstacle to find rare animals and snag them. Once, to catch a man-eating tiger, he used the remains of the dead man for bait.

Circuses worldwide and many American zoos owe their beginnings to him. In the spring of 1922, he provided Dallas with an entire zoo of over 500 animals and birds. In 1948 he returned to Gainesville to dedicate the Frank Buck Zoo and the Frank Buck Zoological Society. He was driven, he wrote, to seek "the source of the wind, the mouth of the river, the oceans to which the fish swam, and the far lands and forests to which the birds flew."

It could be said that Buck had birds on the brain. In fact, he chose them over his first wife, *Chicago News* drama critic Amy Leslie. Soon after the wedding, he rented a home in the country and filled the property with cardinals, finches, teals, orioles, English swans, and peafowl. The bride was a "city girl" and preferred the plumage of ball gowns and a menagerie of stage sophisticates to the aviary he was assembling in the backyard.

"I loved every feather on those fowl," he wrote, and the glitter of the Chicago nightlife was dull to him when compared with "the sheen of their proud backs."

So she didn't try to stop him when he told her in 1911 that he was using $3,500 he had won in a card game to go to South America. He would bring back the birds he had read about in the library. This is what he wrote in his autobiography. We can only guess at her side of the issue. She may have given him the money to get rid of him—and his birds.

She was wise, in any case, to let him go, as a husband who seeks the source of the wind would be forever restless, especially in the windy city. She must have known that the only home he wanted was the jungle.

Dallas had been his childhood home after his family left Gainesville, and the Turtle Creek area, only a few blocks from downtown, became his first jungle. He wasn't a boy to like school, insufficient as it was in bird population. Geography thrilled him but the other subjects sent him into daydreams of claw and feather. He regularly hookied away to the creek to commune with the creatures, then fetch them home in sacks. The first snake he brought home his mother dispatched with a garden hoe. Another lifelong lesson learned: Always safeguard your animals.

She was a good parent, though, as was his father, a tough hombre with a gentle soul. But the exotic places in the geography books pulled the bird-boy and, as soon as he was old enough, he took flight.

It was not the wind but the rails he followed to Chicago. To pay his way he punched cows, forcing them into railroad cars by punching them with the nail in the end of a stick. In Chicago, he soon trapped the drama critic, using his astonishing good looks as bait. The marriage propelled him into the headlines for the first time—*Amy Leslie Marries Bellboy!* She proposed, he wrote.

With her advantage of an education and fifteen years in age, she was a female Pygmalion. "Ain't" and other crudities were soon replaced with sophisticated lingo and fancy attire. She introduced him to important people, and he became a vaudeville manager, then a theatrical correspondent. To promote their Galateas, Pygmalions use their powers shamelessly.

But from the instant he first set his boot sole in the jungle, he said he was happy for the first time in his life. "I decided then, there, and permanently, while the tropical sun beat down and heavy foliage steamed," he wrote, "that the jungles of the world were my future life and that from them in some way I should earn my living." During the succeeding three decades he captured 100,000 birds, sixty-five tigers, fifty elephants, many rhinos, hippos, primates of every variety, deer, buffalo, snakes—a seemingly endless catalogue of wild animals, crated and shipped back for sale to zoos, circuses, and private collectors. Noah would be flooded, so to speak, with envy.

He made $3,000 profit on his first expedition, but he profited more by his random meeting with the famed promoter Tex Rickard, outside a Buenos Aires movie house. They had been the only Americans watching the film of the Jack Johnson-James Jeffries fight. Rickard had been the referee in that fight as well as the promoter. They became friends, and from this master of media manipulation Buck learned the art of self-promotion. He parlayed his animal expertise into shows at world's fairs, Madison Square Garden, and Radio City Music Hall. He made "B-movies" with titles like *Jungle Menace, Wild Cargo*, and *Bring 'em Back Alive*. For twenty-four weeks, he even substituted for *The Amos 'n' Andy Show* on radio, earning $2,000 a week—big money back then.

His headquarters in the Far East became the Raffles Hotel in Singapore. From here, his collecting network spread to India, Borneo, Sumatra, Malaya—all the jungles of Asia. The Raffles was in those days a gathering place for international travelers, idle rich, and dealers in exotic Eastern commodities of all kinds. It was here that a murder, said the police, occurred, and Buck was the prime suspect. After a party, the body of one of the men in attendance was found on the pavement directly beneath Buck's third-floor room. The police suspected that the man had come there looking for his wife and that Buck had thrown him out the window. The police knew that on the day before, Buck had pummeled a "Dutchman" for spreading the rumor that Buck was sparking another man's wife. Nevertheless, the coroner ruled it "death by misadventure"; and the freedom of the world's animals, not Buck's, was again in jeopardy.

At the height of his fame, he married Muriel Riley in California and bought a home in the San Fernando Valley. He filled immense aviaries on the estate with Australian parakeets, fairy bluebirds from Malaysia, cockatoos, pheasants, and African touracos. He planned to sit back and relax to the trill of their songs. In all, he spent less than a month there. When adventure called—world's fairs, movie openings, speaking engagements, circuses, expeditions—he could never resist.

Only death could still him. He died in Houston, March 25, 1950.

There is something of a taint today on the idea of trapping animals, and there are laws governing dealing in them. Though Buck never killed or even harmed an animal except in self-defense, he lost many to disease and captivity before he could get them to buyers. Once, all the animals on deck, virtually his entire cargo, drowned in a typhoon. He profited in a profession that has lost its appeal. Some people are repulsed by the way he earned his living and by circuses and zoos in particular. But when he is assayed against the backdrop of the cruelty of his times, he could be viewed as a pioneer in animal preservation.

He may have been the most famous Texan of his day, but he wasn't a cowboy. His celebrity has waned partly because of the ascendance of the Texas myth of cowboys and cattle trails. He captured animals for captivity, but the animals the revered cowboy rounded up and herded into boxcars ended up in the slaughterhouse. To me, growing up on the wrong side of the Santa Fe railroad tracks in a small Texas town, Frank Buck's life meant that any boy, even one born in a Gainesville wagonyard, could dare to do big things.

· · · ❦ · · ·

# Give Me That Old Time Mythology

Big Tex is the first thing you see when you enter the main gate at the State Fair. On the surface, you might think he's just another 52-foot-tall cowboy wearing a 75-gallon hat and a pair of size 70 boots. Or that he is just a meeting place for fair-goers. A pick-up site for lost children: "If you get lost, go to Big Tex and wait till I find you."

Big Tex is deeper than this, though. To those who suggest updating him to suit the times, I say he's complicated—and no one who understands what myth is and our relationship to it would ever try to change him. The notion that he is no longer representative of Texas and should be updated proceeds from the assumption that there ever *was* a time when he represented what Texas *actually* was. He's not just a big dumb cowboy that only other big dumb cowboys look up to, so to speak. There aren't that many cowboys in Texas anyway—and never have been, any more than in other western states, anyway. I have lived in Texas all my life but have never had the pleasure of meeting a *real* cowboy. My horsemanship has been restricted mainly to the carousel. My life, like that of most Texans, has always been associated with cars and freeways and office work and bureaucracy and suburbs and football games and shopping malls and backyard barbecues— but, like everyone else, I would like for it to be *more* than this.

221

Big Tex embodies this dream. He is an icon of the hero myth, in this case, the cowboy hero. Texas business leaders and promoters hot for the dollar exploited this image of Texas early in this century, and the movies gave it permanence in the American consciousness. I saw John Wayne portraying Texas cowboys so many times on screen that I thought he actually was one. But of course, he was neither a cowboy nor a Texan. I realized this when I heard him pronounce *rodeo* as *ro-day-o*. No real Texan would ever do that. But I liked him anyway as a Texas cowboy because it was the myth he represented that was important, not the reality.

It isn't that we would *really* like to be cowboys—they ride hard in the saddle all day long in all kinds of weather and eat beans and sleep on the ground. That is not it at all. It is the cowboy's *freedom* we hanker for. Just listen to the cowboy songs—they're all about living free, punching cattle not a time clock, roaming across the wide open spaces beneath the starry skies above, gazing at the moon until we lose our senses. Getting back in the saddle again and riding along the trail to wherever it takes you, with your spurs going jingle jangle jingle. You can do anything to me but don't fence me in.

We look at Big Tex and are brought together in this common dream of freedom, of a life of feelings, a life of the heart where, as the song says, "the only law is *right*." This is what myths do.

That Texas is becoming one of the high-tech centers of America, that it is now mostly urban, multilingual, and has strong elements of feminism—does, in fact, signal a transition for us in the twenty-first century. There are many more Texans by far employed in the high-tech industry than in the Texas ranching industry. But, again, this is not the point. When myth and fact collide, myth wins every time. Make Big Tex a multilingual, technocrat and dress him in high water pants, blue double-knit shirt with a plastic pen-guard in the pocket, and replace his longhorn belt buckle with a computer monitor and you have made him politically correct and representative of a large segment of Texas culture, but you have also eliminated the point of having him in the first place.

No one yearns to leave all his troubles behind and go off and become a systems analyst.

R.L. Thorton, a genius by today's standards, knew what he was doing when he invented Big Tex in 1951. Post-war Texas was hardly half-rural by this time, and this meant farm-rural, not ranch-rural. He was after a myth, not diversity. Diversity in those days meant three Protestant denominations tolerating each other in the same town. Mr. Thornton knew that the only thing better than a myth is a giant myth, so he bought a colossal Santa Claus from Kerens, Texas, for $750, and made him into Big Tex, a gigantic, transmythical galoot.

Big Tex may be under fire as an icon, but the ideas he represents—freedom, wide-open spaces, and individualism—will be as important in the next century as they ever were, no matter who, or what, symbolizes them.

· · · 🍎 · · ·

# Give Me All Your Dismembered Men

I have a hazy recollection of my mother reading me a story. It was "The Three Little Pigs." Other than this story, that one time, there was no other. My upbringing was far removed from literature, books, and reading. My grandparents' daylight-to-dark toil on rural Texas farms precluded the luxury of an education. My grandmother read only the King James Bible and the *Cleburne Times Review*. The Grand Ole Opry was the extent of their arts and culture. The only books in the household were those I began bringing in when I was ten. Naturally, then, I have often wondered about the source of my love of books and reading.

It occurred to me in one of those reveries we all have, in which a fragrance, a word, a tone, can trigger a remembrance not thought of in years. In this case I was driving, and from the radio I heard the words "red-headed man." Instantly, I was a child again and playing a card game with my cousins. It was a game called "Authors." It probably doesn't exist anymore, because of the change in society's values.

In any case, when cousins Janie and Kathleen came to visit from Houston, we played this game—with the zeal kids nowadays play video games, I suppose. It was played like "Old Maid," the object being to collect "books," that is, all four cards, of as many as possible of these authors: Poe, Irving, Shakespeare, Tennyson, Twain, Alcott, Cooper, Whitman, Longfellow, Scott, Stevenson, Dickens, and Hawthorne. Below the picture of each author was a list of the author's greatest books. I was in elementary school and could read. My cousins could not yet but made do by holding up the cards they wanted. Hence, Hawthorne was the "red-headed man"; Louisa May Alcott was "the old woman"; and due to his look, I suppose, of arrested puberty, Sir Walter Scott was "the little boy." This is called kid logic and is not to be questioned.

Our game of "Authors" usually began with Kathleen saying, "Let's play 'Ossus,'" which was about as close as she could come to the word. Oh the times we had, vying for "the old woman," or the "red-headed man!" By the end of their visit those cards were raggedy but intact. Somehow, we managed to keep up with them until we wore them out.

When disputes arose, adults did not intervene and we haggled until we managed to work them out among ourselves.

This reverie prompted me to look for this game for my grandchildren, but no store had it. No one had ever heard of it. There were countless video games, of course, most of them centering on violence. Of low-tech games there was "Clue," about solving murders, and "Monopoly," to teach children the tactics for acquiring money and property. But no "Authors," a simple game which teaches only the classics of literature.

Is this game the basis for my urge toward books and reading? In elementary school, I knew all these authors and what they wrote because I had memorized the lists of their books beneath their pictures on the cards. Kathleen now lives in Palm Springs and has a bookstore. Janie is a lover of books and has read widely.

I was a literature teacher.

This game evidently shaped our values. I hope the boys and girls today who play "Doom" and "Duke Nukem" with the fervor with which we played "Authors" are not so strongly and lastingly influenced.

· · · ❧ · · ·

# The Little Trolleys That Might Could

Road crews excavating Highway 67 for widening between Cleburne and Alvarado found two streetcars inside one of the houses. These weren't miniatures of old trolleys like the ones sold for display. Oh no. These were electric streetcars, forty feet long, with "Dallas Railway Terminal" still visible on the sides.

The trolleys were bought in 1966 by Alvarado native Christine Littleton's father for $250 each. Then Christine and her husband, Ray, added walls and a roof and lived in them for twelve years. Later, they built a house behind, where they've lived ever since.

I went along with Fort Worth *Star-Telegram* columnist Jon McConal and sat in on his interview with the Littletons. Mr. Littleton, a part-time Baptist preacher, told us the history of the cars in biblical detail.

Later I went over and rode the McKinney Avenue trolley, similar to the ones found. Longtime KERA listener Pat Bosko, who operates it on Tuesdays and Thursdays, invited me. In the trolley barn I spoke with volunteer Steve Reed, who said that these discovered cars should be restored and placed back into operation in Cleburne, where the old Interurban tracks still exist. "Can you imagine the new life these cars would bring to that town?" he said. "They attract tourists like magnets."

True, said operator Mike Russell, but city politicians are reluctant to fund trolley restoration. "In our case," he went on, "they were opposed to it until it became so popular and revitalized this whole area. Now, they take credit for it."

John Landrum, who oversees the restoration of the McKinney Avenue trolleys, knew about the discovery. He showed me one similar and another, a much larger Interurban car being restored which will be a dining car and on the McKinney track in a year or so. It had been used as a hay barn in Granbury for fifty-eight years. The cat named Handley that I saw lying in the water fountain was one of three unweaned kittens workers found beneath the floor. Sister Melissa was given away, John said, and that would be Sherman over there sleeping on the red velvet seat of the trolley.

Andy Nold, who is helping restore two Interurban cars in Fort Worth, drove to Alvarado to view the cars. They're numbers 415 and 424, he said, built in St. Louis in the nineteen-teens and used in Dallas until 1954. They're in good condition because they were inside that house all those years, except that 415 has a big chunk cut out of the side. He recommends that Cleburne restore 424 by using all the good parts from 415.

For a hundred years, Cleburne was one of the railroad centers of Texas before the Santa Fe pulled out in 1986. The Interurban ran through there from 1912 to 1930. Now, by returning to its past, the town has a chance to renew itself in a new century.

$$\bullet \ \bullet \ \bullet \ \text{🐛} \ \bullet \ \bullet \ \bullet$$

# Dead Preachers Society

I've always wanted to sit in on a lecture by a dead author and get an autograph. So when I read in the Midlothian *Today* newspaper that Mary Baker Eddy would be lecturing and autographing at Walden Books in Cleburne, I jump-started the pickup.

But first I called the paper to make sure the noted founder of the Christian Science religion would, in fact, be in Cleburne at the advertised time. Brian Porter, *Today* reporter, told me that his paper had gotten the story as a news release and printed it. As far as he knew, he said, Mrs. Eddy would show up and would be signing autographs.

Well, I had studied about Mrs. Eddy in college and remembered that she was a contemporary of Mark Twain and that he had written a book about Christian Science. Ironically, they died in the same year, 1910. *If* she died. Her belief, as I remember it, was based on the idea that death does not exist as we know it.

If she was right, a book signing in Cleburne would not be out of the question. In any case, she couldn't be deader than some of the authors I've seen at these events. I dug out my camera. But would she show up on film? I bought the fastest film Eckerd's had.

The sign at the entrance to the Nolan River Mall in Cleburne did, in fact, state it in big letters: MARY BAKER EDDY LEC-TURING AND AUTOGRAPHING HER BEST-SELLING BOOK SCIENCE AND HEALTH APRIL 10.

Store employee Dorothy Brooks said that it was a typographical error by their advertising department, that Mrs. Eddy was deceased and would not be coming. I was disappointed but not surprised. Being dead is so detrimental to an author's speaking tour that even a marketing genius cannot overcome it. Frank Sinatra is said to have considered death such a bad career move for him that he asked his family not to tell anybody about it when he died.

I asked Dorothy whether she intended to amend the sign to indicate that Mrs. Eddy was deceased and would not be showing up. She said that I was the only person to be so worked up about it.

Well, in that case, I said, maybe next week she could advertise a personal appearance of Christopher Columbus, lecturing and autographing his book *Famous Sea Voyages I've Had*.

She laughed good-naturedly and said she had a better idea. "Why don't you come in and autograph your own book?"

"Do you think a live author would go over in this town?" I said.

"Sure, why not?" she said.

I said okay, since it is my hometown. But I'm a little uncomfortable with an invitation from a bookstore that specializes in autograph parties for dead authors.

# Picking Up Robert

The weekend of Robert Murray's forty-second birthday, eldest son Lindon made one of his many trips to Decatur to pick him up and bring him to his house in Midlothian. They've been close friends since rehab, seventeen years ago. Like all close friends, they share common interests. They go to rock concerts, stock car races, and air shows. They enjoy shooting black powder rifles and watching *Andy Griffith*.

Robert is easy-going and, if stretched out, would be long and languorous, like his West Texas lingo. He has a tough and bright personality that makes everyone feel at ease. He has had more than his share of hardship since graduating from Lefors High School. I could tell from the way he was reminiscing that he has reached that common age when everyone faces that dread "Things Haven't Worked Out as Planned" syndrome.

For Lindon, who's thirty-eight and will be reaching his own midlife crisis in a few years, Robert is a good model. He's optimistic, totally free of bitterness, and doesn't whine. Since he has no job or ex-wives, you might think he would have nothing to talk about but he does. He has the most interesting topic in the world to discuss—the doings of the person he's talking to. The person who is interested in others never wants for conversation.

When Robert spends the weekend, Lindon undresses him and helps him into bed. Lindon's brother Lowell lives around the corner and comes by in the mornings and helps Robert get out of bed after Lindon has gotten him dressed. I do it when Lowell is not available. There's a pattern to it. You place his wheelchair beside the bed, then pull him straight up into a sitting position. Next, you move his legs around until they're hanging off the bed and he's facing you. He puts his arms around your neck and holds tight while you grasp him around the waist and lift him up and around and into his chair.

Lindon wishes he could do this for Robert. He's strong enough, but sitting in a wheelchair himself, he can't raise Robert high enough to transfer him into his chair. Even Bob Caudle (Casey), their pal who has a low-level injury and can do almost anything, can't do that. You have to be able to stand up to do it. Casey can do things, however, that seem wondrous to Robert and Lindon. He can pull himself up by the fender well of a car and hold on with one hand and work on the engine with the other. This is a big deal. Lindon was an expert mechanic but is now able to repair only the things he can reach while sitting down. He gets on his back on a creeper, his wheelchair tied to his foot to keep it with him, and can work underneath cars. But he has to rely on others to bring him tools. It's important not to have to rely on anyone.

Everyone has gotten used to the fact that Lindon is going to keep driving to Decatur to get Robert. He won't bother with a cell phone. We worry that something will go wrong. I suggested that he take someone with him when he makes these long trips. Soon after that, he called and said he had just come back from getting Robert and had broken a fan belt on the way. Luckily, he said, he had an extra in the trunk and was back on the road in no time.

"I guess you took my advice and carried someone with you," I said.

"Sure, Dad," he said, "I took Casey with me."

# Reading For Freedom

What great luck, attending two library sociables in one week! One I went to as a guest of Bob Compton, a champion of reading in Texas. For years, as book editor of the *Dallas Morning News*, he decided which of the hundreds of books that crossed his desk each week would get reviewed. Many of those that didn't he donated to the library at Teague.

On this particular day he brought six boxes. Teague is his hometown, and he's more popular there than Mrs. Baird's bread. Librarians Doris Harrington and Nancy Roberts greeted him with the ceremony that small towns usually reserve for football coaches. This affection for things literary shows in their newspaper. Reporter Margaret Bogue wrote a prizeworthy account of the event. The quality of her writing should shame many big-city reporters. She learned writing in the days before reporters became addicted to cliches.

Later that week I attended the Dallas Public Library's annual Friends of the Library banquet as guest of library friend Barbara Munford. Though literacy be a vagrant today, libraries are its haven. Each year the Friends of the Library raise money for books and other library necessities with these sociables. One way is by bringing in luminaries of the leaf to speak and autograph their books. This time it was Elmer Kelton, the genuine silk elastic of western fiction. He has won six Spur Awards and four Western Heritage awards. *The Good Old Boys* is his most famous, because it was made into a movie by Tommy Lee Jones. *The Year it Didn't Rain* is the one he believes is his masterpiece, however. Out soon will be *The Buckskin Line*.

In his remarks, he told of a country boy's love of books and libraries. I gathered from what he said that he read books because he felt the need to do so—not to win school contests or even to get good grades.

I understand completely. Reading for me was an involuntary action. Actually, I think I could have made better grades if I had read less. I read so many books I liked that I had little time left to read the ones my teachers assigned—which I usually didn't like. The only way I would have read more books is if they had been banned.

In fairness to today's youth, when we were growing up there were fewer distractions—although we had radio and movies. Today, of course, there are these but also television, the Internet, and computer games. I think libraries make a mistake by trying to compete with these by saying that reading is fun. If reading were fun, everybody would be doing it, especially kids. People who read do so because they want to learn about themselves and others and the world around them. Great books are mirrors that we look into to see who we really are. For a lot of people, I suspect, this would not be fun. We are what we read.

Libraries should say that reading great books is the only road to truth. Great books liberate readers from the bonds of conventional wisdom promoted by the marketplace. Movies are viewed by control groups and changed according to their tastes. What is taught in schools is subject to the approval of parents. Ratings and sponsors dictate that television shows be directed to the lowest common level. Preachers and politicians don't want to offend anyone with a heavy purse.

Books cover every conceivable subject and are not censored. Classics, not barbells, should be encouraged in prisons. Convicts passing exams over the world's great classics should be allowed to graduate with a certificate of wisdom.

Who knows? Maybe this idea would spread to the schools.

# The Hieroglyphics of Spanky

I tried not to go sappy when Spanky died, but she had been with us for a long time, and anyone who has ever had a pet for nearly twenty years knows how that feels. Cats are sometimes considered a part of the family, though they have actually lost status since Egyptian days when they were worshiped. They ate the rats that ate the grain, and the penalty for killing one was death. I saw this on the Discovery channel, I think. When the household cat died, the owners shaved off their eyebrows and went into a period of official mourning. It was elaborately mummified and buried in a cat coffin in a sacred cemetery. In the nineteenth century, the British excavated hundreds of thousands of them and ground them up for fertilizer.

When I woke up and Spanky was dead, I would have shaved off my eyebrows if it would have made me feel any better. I wrapped her up in newspaper and laid her in a small grave in the backyard and tried not to cry by reminding myself that she was better off. Her kidneys had shut down at the last. She couldn't eat, and petting her was like passing your hand over a skeleton. She began to look eerily like a snake.

I couldn't bury her beside Cindy and Four because hedges grow there now. Besides, they were dogs, and she never liked them.

Though she was certainly no Democrat, she was born when Carter was president and died during the Clinton administration. She was an aristocrat cat. She was dark brown on one side of her face and light brown on the other—not exactly beautiful but pretty enough to get pregnant before her first birthday and have five kittens. After her operation, she went the rest of her life without sex and became very imperial. The entire house was her domain, and she conveyed this to other cats that came and went along the way. She never acknowledged them except to spit when they came near her. She had little use for the hoi cattoi.

She particularly disdained Four, a dog we had for fourteen years that resembled a pig. She may have thought he was a pig because she wouldn't eat from her bowl if his lips had touched it. He used to lie in my lap and watch television. She bided her time, and when he died she took over his place. She especially enjoyed the Disney channel when there was a good movie on, like *The Lady is a Tramp*. She liked the Discovery channel and National Geographic specials as long as there were no lions or tigers being harmed.

Toward the end she couldn't groom herself very well, and I wouldn't let her sit with me because of her aroma. No big deal. She just waited till I dropped off to sleep. When I woke up, there she was.

The first night of watching TV without her was hard, but now we have Toonses, a Siamese mixture who also enjoys jungle documentaries. The other night that show about the history of cats came on again, but I clicked it off before it got to the part about grinding them into fertilizer.

## Rounding Up the Usual Suspects

On a regular basis, the *Waxahachie Daily Light*, my county's largest newspaper, reports on a drug raid on its front page. These stories have the same theme—"police on the job," "saving society," "filling the prisons," and so on. For many such small county seats, crime is their leading industry. Not only police officers and deputies owe a part of their livelihood to drug offenders and the continuance of their wrongdoing, but also judges, bail bondsmen, lawyers, bailiffs, dispatchers, constables, and many others.

A recent raid was reported in the January tenth edition. It includes a photo of a young man on his knees, handcuffed in his living room with a young woman standing beside him in her nightgown. "Clothed from head to toe, in black tactical uniforms, several officers made a speedy entry into the small trailer home," the story says. It goes on to describe another raid on a dilapidated house later that evening in which a young woman is arrested and $900 in cash and possible stolen items seized.

These officers are brave for breaking into these hovels in the night. They believe they are soldiers in the war on drugs. But I don't think it is a war on drugs at all. I think it is a war on the poor.

The class bias in drug law enforcement is so blatant that you would think even a small-town newspaper could see it. Assuming that both of these offenders are crack cocaine dealers, their living conditions indicate that they aren't exactly flooding the community with their product. Where do the drug kingpins live? Why not raid their homes? High-level drug entrepreneurs launder their cash through banks. Why not raid the local banks, arrest everyone who has traces of cocaine on their hands, assume they're guilty, and write it up in the paper?

The affluent are seldom arrested, and if they are they hire good lawyers. Statistics gathered by Michael Parenti in *Democracy For the Few* indicate that the underclass go to prison ninety percent of the time without a trial, due to plea bargains struck by public defenders.

Millions of Americans would not take drugs like these if they were free and delivered to their doorsteps. Others of all classes enjoy them and think they should be legal, like alcohol and tobacco. Still others are addicted and will get them despite the laws and despite the punishment. Nothing, not even prison, can stop anyone wanting drugs badly enough.

A few years ago a Waxahachie reserve police officer was caught taking cocaine from the vault, but instead of photographing him handcuffed and on his knees the newspaper treated him sympathetically in a story, and important politicians interceded for him. His was a sad tale of addiction; his family suffered, and he deserved the help he got. But the families of the poor are suffering too.

In the rare instance when drug activity among the affluent is reported in the media, it is after a deadly overdose and then the offenders are treated as victims. They *are* victims, but so are the poor who violate the drug laws, and so are the police officers who lose their lives enforcing them.

· · · ❦ · · ·

# Getting a Railroad Town Back on Track

In the Cleburne City Park, passenger locomotive 3417 stands silently against a backdrop of families picnicking and children throwing Frisbees. This is a setting that is alien to her. Her proper environment is the open track as she screeches, rumbles, and roars along the main line, her boiler red-hot and her stack billowing steam against the sky. Her enormous, graceful mass is shaped and balanced for speed and power. Yet she stands there powerless and amidst the mindless frivolity of urban recreationers.

Like the retired crews who graced her cab, she was once an important part of the Santa Fe's operation in the north-central Texas town of Cleburne. The railroad was the lifeblood of the town's economy for over a century. In 1950, the heyday for Cleburne's repair shop, it repaired more than 500 engines and 6,000 boxcars. It had a payroll of six million dollars and employed over 1,500. It paid $50,000 in taxes to the city for its 232-acre facility and 67 miles of track. In 1984, its last big year, the shop payroll was $21 million, and a work force of 750 repaired and serviced 638 locomotives. Since 1946 it had been the largest repair shop on the Santa Fe's southern line.

Santa Fe was a name in my life with pervasive and encompassing implications. I received the foundation for my education at Santa Fe Elementary. At Cleburne High School, our yearbook was "The Santa Fe Trail." In the summer fast-pitch softball leagues at the city park where Santa Fe steam locomotive 3417 now stands on display, I rooted for the Santa Fe "Oilers." The necessities of my youth—food, clothing, shelter, and a Cushman motorscooter—were provided by the paycheck my grandfather brought home every two weeks from the Santa Fe's fire department. The last sounds I heard on summer nights before falling asleep were those of boxcars bumping together in the train yard. I knew there was a job waiting for me out there if I wanted it. A high school pal, Bill Shehorn, who retired this year after forty years as a Santa Fe switchman, told me that the 1956 Cleburne football team had five starters whose fathers worked at the Santa Fe. "Myself," he said, "Bobby Manasco, Gary Whites, Dale McElroy, and Charles Jowell."

I visited with his father, Benson Shehorn, and his breakfast club of retired railroaders down at the Whataburger in Cleburne. They meet there most mornings to talk railroad and run down Republicans. Shehorn is eighty-two but looks, amazingly so, the youngest of the club. That morning they include L.W. Sikes, sixty-five, Homer Hanna, sixty, and Roy Eastus, sixty-four, all retired machinists. "Roy was my apprentice boy," said Shehorn.

"I broke him in right but he went haywire later." Railroaders make with the jokes a lot.

For some reason, no one seems to know why, the Santa Fe closed down its Cleburne shops in the 1980s and left. There are several theories about this, ranging from the city's increasing tax gouging, to the whimsical, vengeful act of a visiting high-ranking railroad official who was mistreated by the Cleburne police. This latter tale, which meets all the requirements of an urban myth, is usually told in whispers. But whatever explanation you choose, there's no getting around the fact, says Shehorn Sr., that it happened during a Republican administration. "It was the worst thing that ever happened to this town," he goes on.

"If it hadn't been for the railroad, Cleburne wouldn't be what it is today," says Sikes. "You'd go into these stores here to buy something on credit and they'd ask you where you worked and if you said the railroad, that was all you had to say."

"You came out of high school with no training for anything," adds Eastus, "and the Santa Fe took you in as an apprentice and you made more money than a lot of people made with college educations. We even had some college graduates come to work there in the backshop."

"I heard a lot of men get up on the facing plate [a heavy steel block railroaders used as a podium to deliver their retirement orations] and talk about what the railroad meant to them," says Hanna, "but I really didn't realize how good it had been to me till it was my turn. The railroad educated my children. It fed my family. It still does. If I had worked in some other industry, I wouldn't be able to do what I do in my retirement."

"We'd be hello guys out here at Wal-Mart," says Shehorn.

"It's nice to see that y'all still get together this way," I say, as I was leaving.

"Railroaders, you know, just naturally like to be together," Shehorn says.

I had an appointment with Jon McConal of the Fort Worth *Star-Telegram*, who was writing a column on the "Club Domino," the hangout where another group of retired railroaders meet to slam the ivory down and otherwise get loud and dreadful. Club regulars include engineers Eli Cooper and John Donoho, and carman Carl Glenn. On this day, there are some regular people there for the mayhem. Finis Carper, C.E. Kennedy, and Bob Middleton, not railroaders but just as rowdy, toil mightily in a cut-throat game in which no one's feelings or family history is spared if a questionable play is made.

Club Domino, as Cooper calls it, is actually a small room on the north side of the Greenbriar Inn. It has just enough space to accommodate two tables, eight chairs, and a space heater. An ancient air conditioner cools things down in the blistering summers. Its décor you might call yard office retro-grunge. Noel White leases the space to "provide a place for all of us to hang out and get out of our wives' hair," he says. He's a relative youngster, forty-eight, who left his machinist's job at the railroad after seventeen years and started his cement-cutting business. The men drop money into the kitty to pay for the lease and utilities.

I didn't recognize Cooper as he kibitzed the game. The passage of forty years has altered our appearances somewhat. I introduced myself to the boys, adding, "I'm a friend of Eli Cooper, but I hope you won't hold that against me."

A tall, white-haired gent gets up and extends his hand. "Are you Eli?" I deadpan. "I need some identification. The real Eli Cooper has a stub finger on his left hand."

"It hasn't grown back!" he says, holding up the stub.

Later on, I tell McConal how I recognized Cooper.

"How did you lose that finger, Eli?" McConal says, setting up the gag as smoothly as if it had been rehearsed.

"I was picking my nose and a booger bit it off," Cooper says, without missing a beat. The club members ignore this punch line. They've heard it too many times before.

Cooper, seventy-two, and Donoho, seventy-five, are two of the youngest members of an elite group in Cleburne. They are steam engineers. When they hired out in 1947, steam engines were still the workhorses of the railroad's fleet but were running on borrowed time. Other surviving steam engineers in Cleburne include Buddy Corzine, G. V. Pritchard, and J. E. Goodale, all in their eighties. There are very few others. They're not sentimental about 3417. They agree that diesels are much more comfortable. "Steamers were rough-riding and rattled and clattered," Cooper says. "And they were hot in the summer and cold in the winter." But they were faster than diesels. "I've been on one going 105 miles an hour," he says.

The boys are domino mavins and uninterested at the moment in speculating on anything other than the other guy's hand. So I don't interrupt their game to ask about the demise of the Santa Fe in Cleburne and its effect on the town.

Someone who does have such opinions is Bill Miller, who owns the bookstore one block away on South Main Street. He is something of a railroad historian and, at sixty-four, remembers the steam era in its heyday. "The Santa Fe bankrolled this town for decades," he says. "There were no other good jobs here, and it seems like not enough people here really appreciated it till it was gone." He wants a railroad museum in the town that would draw tourists. He supports the renovation of 3417 but is skeptical of the town leaders' interest. "We had four railroads here at the turn of the century and the town hasn't ever capitalized on that," he says.

There is a campaign in Cleburne, led by Mike Percifield, a railroad enthusiast, for the engine's renovation. But $25,000 is needed, he says, to remove the asbestos from the cab before any other work can begin. An influential supporter is W. F. (Dub) Stepp, a retired general foreman. He worked on 3417 in his early years as a machinist. Like many others in town, his is a family of railroaders. His father was a carman. W. F. Jr., is an engineer in Fort Worth. His daughter Candy Sossamon was an extraboard clerk from 1976 to 1987. "That locomotive made a living for a lot of people in this town," he says succinctly.

Town leaders think first about the money involved, of course. But few paid consultants would be needed. The brainpower is there in the heads of all its retired steam engineers, boilermakers, electricians, and machinists. Boilermaker W. O. Parnell, who hired out in 1942, is very familiar with 3417. He says he "worked on it, in it, under it, and all through it" and, like the others, is eager to help in any way he can

The Santa Fe left town a dozen years ago, but memories of it are vivid among its older townspeople and especially in the minds of its retired employees. Those who toiled on the old steamers make up a small group that is getting smaller. There can never again be such a group. Like passenger engine 3417, ignored and deteriorating, they are monuments to a simpler, some say, nobler, era. They wish the town would somehow honor that era.

As long as they are wishing, let them wish for a miracle: that 3417's boiler will fire once again and steam will rise from her stack as she highballs down the main line, her cars filled with happy, deep-pocketed tourists, the jingle of cash registers making music in the hearts of merchants and town leaders. Then, by returning to its past, Cleburne might go forward into a new century—by recapturing the glory of its railroad history.

Meanwhile, in the park, the engine waits.

# Unlucky Dog

Nipper is a blue heeler, known as a cow dog because, like others of his breed, he likes to herd cattle. Only there were no cows where he was living when I first made his acquaintance. He was hanging out at the track behind the Midlothian High School beneath some framed tires the football boys somehow use for practice.

He growled and blustered at my dog Tipper when we jogged by his turf. But it was only an act, of course. After this little display was over, he followed us around the track, nipping harmlessly at my heels. I was the only cow he had at the time, and the track would have to do for a pasture. But in the evenings when the sun went down, the track was full of people-cows for him to herd.

I hoped that someone would take him, but no one ever did. A blue heeler wouldn't win any beauty contests. And, although Texas is supposed to be full of cattle ranches, you have to go a long way from where I live to find a cow. So Nipper didn't have a very bright future.

I had been bringing him food and water every day when we came to jog. I hoped that we could leave it at this arrangement, but he eventually followed me home. Brenda Dodge said the same thing she always says when I spot a wandering dog: "That dog belongs to somebody." I promised, as always, that his stay was only temporary. As for Tipper, he laid down the turf rules immediately: "You can eat my leftovers when I'm done," he said in dog, "but keep your cow-herding lips off of my chew toys!" Of course, he was obliged to emphasize this with a behind-beating or two, but it was soon settled and there was tranquillity.

Until Brenda came home and saw Nipper with one of her new solar-powered outdoor yard lights in his mouth, preparing to use it for a chew toy.

"I want that dog gone by the time I get home tonight," she hinted.

An ad in the Midlothian paper had brought no results. So, I went into the Yellow Pages and came up with the ideal solution: the Ellis County Animal Shelter in Red Oak, a no-kill shelter. I called and got directions. Then we set out, Tipper, old Nipper, and me.

It was not as ideal as I had expected—one woman, Laurie Thompson, the shelter manager, and a young girl in a modular office building with an outdoor kennel beneath the trees. But they had a cage ready for him and it was clean. I gave her a hundred dollars, signed a form, and left. He barked when he heard my truck start up, and I thought I heard him barking all the way home.

He will be adopted, I told myself. Some rancher will be glad to get him. This thought consoled me.

Comes now a news story in the *Waxahachie Daily Light* that the Red Oak shelter will have to close its doors in a month if it doesn't raise at least $5,000. Although the shelter has placed over 2,000 pets in homes, it still has many that haven't been adopted. One of these is a blue heeler named Nipper, who is desperately seeking cows—but in a pinch will herd people.

# Fort Worth's Man of Letters

Poetry is so embedded in our psyches that we are hardly aware of it. Without it we would be all but mute. It is in our cliches. "It's raining cats and dogs," we say, referring to a time in the distant past when pets actually fell through poorly-thatched roofs during hard rains.

"Edgar Allan Poe is a true poet, but rap is just noise," says the high-minded professor, blind to the possibility that "The Raven" might be a rap song for the morbidly brokenhearted.

"I hate poetry," says the boot-scooter as he gallops across the dance floor, the plaintive lyrics of Willie Nelson in his ear.

"Poetry's for girls," says the football fan, swelling with emotion at the sound of "The Star Spangled Banner."

Once, poetry was the people's entertainment before universities and professors appropriated it for themselves. Rather than viewing a poem as a living thing of beauty for all, too many professors attack it as a trophy animal to kill and display for succeeding generations of scholars.

Fortunately, the literary taxidermists have not yet discovered William Barney. His poems were not in their graduate school textbooks. But he is a gifted poet, a true man of letters. In fact, he was a postal inspector for the railroad for many years. His artistry is mystery-born, springing from the same source as that which fired those other great poets of the people, Burns, Whitman, and Shakespeare. If I knew what it was, I would tap into it myself.

Barney is the author of over a dozen books of poetry, most of them literary prize-winners. Once, he won the Robert Frost Award for Poetry, given to him by Frost himself. He has been the Poet Laureate of Texas.

He is eighty-one now and still writing. His new book *A Cowtown Chronicle*, published by Browder Springs Press, honors Fort Worth, his hometown. In it are poems about such interests as rodeos, western paintings and music, landmarks, parades, and wildlife. Some are new and some are among his best from the past.

Aspiring poets should strive for a fraction of Barney's skill in form and diction. His knowledge is deep and broad and, as poetry, becomes wisdom. "Memory won't hold all the store," he writes.

> *How do we ever assimilate*
> *The artifacts and the knowledge,*
> *The passions of time and the arts?*
> *They stir in the mind, they move about,*
> *they settle into solitary spaces.*
> *We never know for sure all they mean,*
> *Though we seek inward to remember.*

In a time of hyperbole and gross self-promotion, Barney's humility is a remnant from a lost but not forgotten world. As a poet, he knows mankind's limitations as well as his own. He knows that poetry is what can't be done: "There are as many ways to grasp the world," he writes,

> *As there are men. More subtleties*
> *of hand, of eye, imagination,*
> *than imagination itself takes measure of,*
> *than eye or ear can hope to record,*
> *or hand, though it strive, ever set down.*

And, on that note of human limitation, these verses from one of the most stirring of all the poems in the book—"A Carol of the Gift of God":

*How can it be, the force that gave*
*both time and space their powers—*
*how can it stoop to bind itself,*
*inhabit flesh like ours?*

*Come Brothers, Sisters, sing for joy!*
*The Gift of God made known*
*Is wrapped in tissue and in trim*
*As mortal as our own.*

The End

# Index